For Maureen and Tom

ACKNOWLEDGEMENTS

John Gaffney, Ken McKone, Charles Telling, Ron Fulbirg, Sylvia Goss, Peter Robson, John Morris, Gordon Lilley, John Goymer, Les Mann, Linda Nicholson, Olive Curry, Fred Stobbart, Jack Jacques, Sadie Smith, Clive and Brenda Parker, Alex Price, Gordon Clark, Tommy Jackson, Detective Constable George Virtue, Cecil Emmerson, Diane Simpson.

Thanks

My thanks to all of the above and to the many Northumbria and West Yorkshire police officers, both serving and retired, who helped with my research but wished to remain anonymous. Thanks also to the many "suspects" in the Ripper inquiry who contributed their stories but, again, wished not to be named. Thanks also to staff at the *Sunderland Echo*, particularly Lawrence Collins, head of design, for proofreading and technical advice, and Ian Lowes, editorial artist, and Kevin Brady, photographer, for advice on pictures and David Dodds, for his advice on marketing, and for the encouragement given to me by many at the Echo, including Editor Andrew Smith. Final thanks go to the people of the north of Sunderland who were put under the national spotlight as a result of the hoax of the century, but came through it all smiling.

Published by
Northeast Press
Echo House
Pennywell
Sunderland
SR4 9ER

First published 1999

ISBN 0-9519968 - 7 - 8

Newspapers and Journals

The Sunderland Echo
The Northern Echo
The Yorkshire Post
The Yorkshire Evening Press
The Daily Mail
The Lancashire Evening Post

Produced by:
Print Techniques Ltd. Washington.
Telephone: 0191 417 8905

Wearside Jack

The Hunt for the Hoaxer of the Century

By Patrick Lavelle

Wearside Jack

The Hunt for the Hoaxer of the Century

CONTENTS

INTRODUCTION

The brutal murder of a mother-of-two in Preston, Lancashire, the pit village of Castletown in Sunderland and a Top Ten single by an American folk singer in the late 1970s appear to have little in common on the face of it.

But all are linked to one man - Wearside Jack - who carried out the most elaborate and costly hoax this century.

In November, 1975, the battered body of 26-year-old Joan Harrison was found in a disused, lock-up garage in Preston. Mrs Harrison, a familiar figure in the town's pubs and clubs, had recently been living in a hostel for the homeless.

She had been savagely kicked about the head and body at least seven times and, for reasons unknown, her killer had also sank his teeth into her left breast.

Murder squad detectives had little to go on. House-to-house inquiries in the area yielded little information and interviews with Mrs Harrison's associates and relatives threw up few clues as to the identity of her killer.

But forensic tests at the scene of the murder did give police at least two clues; the killer was of a rare blood group and forensic scientists were able to ascertain that the murderer had a gap in his two top front teeth of at least an eighth of an inch.

As usual, police were keeping an open mind in the case, not ruling in or out any possible links with other attacks on women in the Lancashire area or further afield. With few clues to go on it was apparent that the killer would only be caught through hard police work.

Detectives hoped for that one lead that would give them a breakthrough in the inquiry and lead them to the killer or at least a prime suspect. Despite regular appeals for information through the local media and hundreds of man hours spent on the inquiry the breakthrough never materialised.

The file on the murder of Joan Harrison is still open; police never close a murder case. Her killer has never been caught.

But further clues as to the identity of a suspect in the case did emerge in later years as a result of another police inquiry; the biggest manhunt in British criminal history this century - the hunt for the Yorkshire Ripper.

Police were able to establish several facts about the probable killer of Mrs Harrison. They already knew he was of a rare blood group and had a gap in his top two front teeth.

Other inquiries revealed he was aged between 20 and 42, he may have been left-handed, he may have worked in engineering, he was a driver and would have had reason to travel occasionally to and from West Yorkshire.

Two other important facts emerged; one - that he owned a copy of the song by Andrew Gold *"Thank You For Being a Friend"* may, at first, appear inconsequential but, evidentially, for police, that fact was very important. The second fact, which was questioned by some police officers, was that Mrs Harrison's probable killer came from the pit village of Castletown in Sunderland.

A suspect in the Joan Harrison murder case had a copy of the Andrew Gold song. Where he bought it from and whether it was a seven-inch vinyl single, from an LP, or copied on to an audio tape is not known. The same man, it emerged, had a slight speech impediment.

From the many facts police had been able to glean during their inquiries into the Mrs Harrison murder case and inquiries elsewhere - most notably in their hunt for the Yorkshire Ripper - an "offender profile" had been drawn up of her possible killer.

Surely, someone in the close-knit community of Castletown could point police in the direction of this man?

Police were able to draw up a profile of the man from Castletown and link him to the Mrs Harrison murder because it was he who sent them three hoax letters and an audio tape at the height of the hunt for the Yorkshire Ripper.

The hoaxer sent the three taunting letters to police in West Yorkshire in March, 1978 - two were forwarded to police that month - and one in March, 1979. Later, in June, 1979, the Castletown man sent police the infamous *"I'm Jack"* audio tape.

The letters - including the letter which contained the audio tape - all had a Sunderland postmark. At the end of the tape, in which the sender taunted police for not being able to catch him, he played some of the Andrew Gold song *"Thank You For Being a Friend"*.

Forensic examination of saliva on the letters revealed that the sender was of the same, rare, blood group as the killer of Mrs Harrison. In one of the letters the sender told police something about a Ripper murder they believed only the serial killer could know.

The link between the Joan Harrison murder through the forensic evidence, the detailed knowledge the sender of the letters and tape had of the Ripper murders, and the intense pressure from the public on police to catch the Yorkshire Ripper led senior officers in West Yorkshire to come to one decisive conclusion. The letters and tape were sent by THE Yorkshire Ripper.

That decision, we all know now, proved costly and - for probably at least three women - it proved fatal. Police were sent on a wild goose chase in the hunt for the serial killer which cost taxpayers millions of pounds.

The letters and tape had a major impact on so many lives in Sunderland and elsewhere, with mothers "grassing" their own sons; wives telling police their husbands were the man behind the voice on the tape.

But police had got it wrong. The murder of Joan Harrison was not the work of the Yorkshire Ripper. Peter Sutcliffe told the jury at his trial he did not kill Mrs Harrison. Although he has a gap in his teeth, he is not of the same rare blood group as her killer. Many years later he told one of his closest confidantes, Olive Curry, when she visited him at Broadmoor: "I did not kill that girl".

The author of the hoax letters and sender of the bizarre *"I'm Jack"* tape who, arguably, perpetrated the hoax of the century, has never been caught, despite the millions of pounds and millions of man hours spent on the inquiry.

Wearside Jack, as he became known, was also, possibly, the killer of Joan Harrison. His hoax, according to most observers of the case, including senior police officers, cost the lives of three women. For while police were on the trail of a man with a Wearside accent, the real Ripper, who was questioned several times but eliminated because of his broad Bradford dialect, went on to murder his last three victims.

This book examines the massive police hunt for Wearside Jack. Research for it has unearthed details and facts never made public in the last 20 years.

This book was not written with the intention of opening old wounds or causing further distress to the relatives of the Ripper victims. Anyone in search of gory details about the crimes of Peter William Sutcliffe will not find them here. Nor was this book written with the intention of further embarrassing police; top-level inquiries into West Yorkshire Police's handling of the case have been held and blame has been apportioned.

"Wearside Jack: The Hunt for the Hoaxer of the Century", focuses on the impact the inquiry had on ordinary people in Sunderland and, in particular, the dramatic impact it had on the folk of Castletown.

We are approaching the Millennium and, as one of the hundreds of men interviewed by the Ripper police told me: "This is the day and age to settle old debts." Wearside Jack has a massive debt to repay the people of Sunderland. It is time the hoaxer was exposed.

Patrick Lavelle.

June, 1999.

PART ONE

The Ripper from the Wear

CHAPTER ONE

"I'm Jack"

"I'm Jack," said the voice: "I see you are still having no luck catching me."

The voice was taunting, the message chilling, and for two minutes at a Press conference in the Police Academy at Wakefield, West Yorkshire, the police, the media and, later, millions of people across the UK, believed they were listening to the voice of the infamous Yorkshire Ripper.

It was June, 1979, and the Ripper, in the previous four years, had brutally murdered 10 if not 11 women in Leeds, Bradford, Manchester, Huddersfield, Halifax and Preston.

Detectives hunting the serial killer were in no doubt that he would strike again. The voice bellowing out from loudspeakers at the Press conference in Wakefield, they believed, was the voice of the Yorkshire Ripper and the broadcasting of the audio tape he had sent them on radio and television was going to give them the breakthrough they had been waiting for in their long-running and expensive murder inquiry.

The tape was two-minutes long, contained 257 words and "Jack", as he called himself, spoke with a distinctive Wearside accent.

Police were convinced of its authenticity for several reasons.

Firstly, forensic tests at the scene of one of the suspected Ripper killings - in Preston in November 1975 - and forensic analysis of the letter in which the tape was sent revealed both the killer and the sender of the tape were of a rare blood group. They were both B secretors.

Secondly, police had already received three letters from the sender of the tape - two in March, 1978, and one in March, 1979 - which, again, contained claims from the correspondent that he was the Yorkshire Ripper. More importantly "Jack" appeared to know more about the serial murders than had been made public.

For senior investigating officers in West Yorkshire working on the case the established links were good enough. The writer of the letters and sender of the tape was the Yorkshire Ripper, and they needed as much help from the public as possible to bring his near five-year reign of terror in the red light areas of West Yorkshire to a swift end.

Thus, the tape was broadcast across the country in a publicity blitz costing at least £1million - money from the taxpayers' coffers - and police also released samples of the suspect's handwriting.

Someone, somewhere, knew who the man was and every effort was to be made by police to catch the most prolific and sadistic killer Britain had ever seen.

West Yorkshire Assistant Chief Constable George Oldfield, other senior officers, and scores of journalists from newspapers and television companies across the country sat in stunned silence and listened as the tape was played.

"I have the greatest respect for you, George," the voice went on, "but, Lord, you are no nearer catching me now than four years ago when I started. I reckon your boys are letting you down, George, they can't be much good, can they?" George Oldfield sat impassively, listening intently and trying to gauge reaction from the faces of the gathered newsmen.

"The only time they came near catching me was a few months back in Chapeltown, when I was disturbed. Even then it was a uniform copper, not a detective.

"I warned you in March that I'd strike again," said the man with the strong Sunderland accent and a lisp. "Sorry it wasn't Bradford. I did promise you that, but I didn't get there. I'm not quite sure when I will strike again, but it will be definitely some time this year, maybe September or October, even sooner if I get the chance.

"I am not sure where, maybe Manchester. I like it there, there's plenty of them knocking about. They never learn, do they George? I bet you've warned them but they never listen."

A click could be heard now and again in the background to the tape, as if "Jack" was clicking the microphone on and off. Perhaps he was reading from a prepared script?

"At the rate I'm going", he continued, "I should be in the book of records. I think it's 11 up to now, isn't it? Well I'll keep on going for quite a while yet. I can't see myself nicked just yet. Even if you do get near I'll probably top myself first.

"Well, it's been nice chatting to you, George.

"Yours, Jack the Ripper."

"Jack" ended the tape with a postscript for Mr Oldfield. "No good looking for fingerprints. You should know by now it's clean as a whistle. See you soon, bye. Hope you like the catchy tune at the end. Ha, ha."

And so there was a tune, though, it could be argued, it was hardly catchy. It was *"Thank You For Being a Friend"* by the American folk singer Andrew Gold. It was released on September 15, 1978, and made the Top Ten in the UK but, as it was up against *Three Times a Lady* by the Commodores and *Dreadlock Holiday* by 10cc, it was never likely to make the Number One slot.

So there it was. The "breakthrough" in the hunt for Britain's most wanted man had started and police were confident in their own judgement and confident that they would get a result.

Shortly after the Press conference, Mr Oldfield said: "I am convinced this is the man who murdered 11 women."

Asked why he was so convinced, Mr Oldfield said: "Handwriting experts are sure the man who addressed the envelope which contained the cassette was the same person who wrote the previous letters.

"In those previous letters there was information about the murders which could only really be known by the killer. He seems to see it as some sort of duel and I am prepared to duel. There can only be one winner in the end."

Mr Oldfield also said: "I am satisfied that the tape and the three letters are from the same man and it is my belief he is the man we are seeking. There is no doubt he was born in Sunderland or the Sunderland area."

The tape was heard in 15million homes across the UK when it was broadcast on television and radio that Tuesday night. Many more thousands of people across the country would hear the tape when it was broadcast in pubs and clubs on Wearside and repeatedly in radio and television news bulletins. A "Dial-the-Ripper" 'phone line, which people could contact direct to hear the tape, was also set up.

The headline in Sunderland's local evening newspaper, the Sunderland Echo, declared: "Ripper is a Wear Man" and in Leeds The Yorkshire Post proclaimed: "The Voice of the Ripper".

In June, 1979, the voice of Wearside Jack became, arguably, the best known in the country. For the first time since 1973, when the underdogs second division Sunderland AFC beat first division Leeds United in the FA Cup Final at Wembley, Sunderland, again, found itself in the national spotlight.

And on the terraces of the Fulwell End at Sunderland's Roker Park football ground hundreds of fans began chanting, to the tune of *"Land of Hope and Glory"*: "I knarr Jack the Ripper, Jack the Ripper knarrs me (and Leicester)". For Wearside Jack, it appeared, there could be no hiding place.

Under-pressure George Oldfield visited Sunderland the day after the tape was first broadcast to the public. Although the hunt for the Ripper was a West Yorkshire Police inquiry they were to be given all the assistance possible from Northumbria Police.

The Northumbria force had appointed Assistant Chief Constable Brian Johnson to head the inquiry. In Sunderland, the investigation was being headed by Detective Superintendent Peter Docherty, the head of Sunderland CID.

On the ground, Detective Inspector Dave Zackrisson - known as "Zack" by the Sunderland Ripper Squad - led a team of detectives in the hunt for the Ripper and a uniformed sergeant - firstly Sergeant Alex Price - led a team of ten police officers from the Special Patrol Group (SPG) who were carrying out thousands of door-to-door inquiries in the north of Sunderland.

Before the major campaign to publicise the tape, the most persuasive case against its authenticity was prepared by Det Insp Zackrisson. He studied every newspaper article written about the inquiry and was convinced he could prove that anything contained in the letters could have been gleaned from newspaper reports.

A team of 12 detectives from West Yorkshire, led by Detective Superintendent Jack Slater, was to be permanently based in Sunderland. The West Yorkshire team was accommodated during the inquiry at the relatively plush Roker Hotel on the seafront.

Within days, the response to the broadcasting of the Ripper tape was "phenomenal", according to a spokesman for West Yorkshire Police. Thirty police officers, he said, were manning telephones non-stop, taking calls from people who believed they recognised the voice.

By Thursday, June 28, 1979 - two days after the broadcast - 400 calls had been received by police in Sunderland from people who had heard the tape or seen samples of Wearside Jack's handwriting. By the Friday, police nationally had taken 2,500 telephone calls, 560 of them were made to police in the incident room at Sunderland's Gill Bridge Avenue Police Station.

On the same day, the "Dial-the-Ripper" Freephone telephone hotline was launched. And it proved to be a hot line. The Leeds number, on which people could hear the tape for themselves, had been "overloaded" with calls.

Such was the interest in the case that clairvoyant and medium Doris Stokes conducted an experiment that night on the programme Friday Live on the North-East regional television station Tyne Tees Television. The "experiment" aimed to reveal the identity of Wearside Jack. Doris Stokes was interviewed by police the following day.

The Ripper tape had been posted in Sunderland - for the letter in which it was contained had a Sunderland postmark - on or before June 18, 1979. Earlier, on March 23, West Yorkshire Police had received the third in a series of letters from Wearside Jack, the first and second letters were posted in March, 1978. All the letters bore a Sunderland postmark.

The third letter (some of the words were never made public) said:

"Dear Officer,

Sorry I haven't written, about a year to be exact, but I haven't been up north for quite a while. I wasn't kidding last time I wrote ... That was last month, so I don't know when I will get back on the job but I know it won't be Chapeltown, too bloody hot there, maybe Bradford, Manningham. Might write again if up north.

Jack the Ripper.

PS. Did you get the letter I sent to Daily Mirror in Manchester".

In the following months the tape was played at scores of workingmen's clubs across Sunderland, among them the Ivy Leaf Club in Hendon and the Catholic Club in Tatham Street. It was also played at pubs and clubs on council estates in Sunderland, including Pennywell Social Club.

At the time police wanted to reach as many people as possible and the tape was played on the nights that the clubs were expecting their biggest crowds of the week. Although the "turn" (entertainment) for the evening was being interrupted the customers in the clubs listened intently to the tape, even though most of them had heard it before.

I was working behind the bar at the Catholic Club in Tatham Street at the time, and I remember the night distinctly. A hush came over the 250 or so people in the concert room as police officers sat on the stage and told the crowd they were about to begin playing the tape.

The voice was without doubt that of a Sunderland man. It sounded so familiar. As it was played in the Catholic Club, where, usually, comedian Bobby Thompson or a group of singers would normally be on stage rather than police officers, the whole situation, to me, appeared surreal.

Knowing the circumstances behind the release of the tape and having been told the voice was that of the Yorkshire Ripper, as the sound reverberated around the club's concert room it felt so eerie. There was a serial killer in our midst and he could even be a neighbour. The voice, to me and many others, sounded just so ordinary.

As well as in the pubs and clubs of Sunderland, the tape was also played in many of the buildings belonging to the town's largest employers. It was even played to staff at the Sunderland Echo, where at least one man's name had been given to police - by his own mother!

The publicity campaign continued and the names of thousands more "suspects" were added to the files at Sunderland's Gill Bridge Avenue Police Station, where a team of detectives and uniformed officers worked Monday to Friday, nine to five, following up and cross referencing every lead.

The hunt for the Yorkshire Ripper and the hunt for Wearside Jack, for now, were one and the same. For the police working on the case they were hunting a serial killer, not a hoaxer, and for the thousands of people who lived in Sunderland, all strangers were viewed with suspicion. The impact the inquiry had on so many lives is immeasurable.

CHAPTER TWO

Ripper Terror

The Chief Constable of West Yorkshire Police, Ronald Gregory, still had the day-to-day running of the force to consider, and the massive amounts of cash being spent in the hunt for the Yorkshire Ripper had a significant impact on the force's budget.

In April, 1979, at the height of the Ripper inquiry, Mr Gregory had asked his police authority to allow six of his officers to take part in the tenth anniversary celebrations of the official twinning of Leeds with Dortmund in West Germany. With all the media focus on the Ripper killings, the trip would give the force some welcome positive publicity.

Although the Ripper had struck fear into the minds of many people in his home stalking ground, most people in Leeds, Bradford and neighbouring towns were trying to live as normal a life as possible.

On the evening of Wednesday April 4, 1979, many people in Leeds were visiting the ABC Cinema in the town's Vicar Lane to see the highly-acclaimed film *The Deerhunter* starring Robert de Niro. Others were staying at home to watch the start of the new, bizarre, comedy series on BBC 2 starring Spike Milligan, titled Q8.

The Earl of Wharncliffe was in the news. He was on a life-support machine in hospital following a crash between two Ford Cortinas near Barnsley. One woman had died in the horror accident and her husband was critically injured.

Yorkshire beauty queen Julie Moxon had also made the headlines in the Yorkshire Evening Press. She had walked out during the judging of the Miss England competition claiming she did not finish in the last seven because of an allegation she was a vice queen.

As local people read their evening newspaper that night an event that would make the front page of the newspapers the next day was unfolding in a park in Halifax, West Yorkshire. The Yorkshire Ripper had struck again, killing his 11th victim.

Building society clerk Josephine Anne Whitaker, a dark-haired 19-year-old, had been brutally murdered. Her killing bore all the hallmarks of a Ripper murder but forensic tests and a post mortem examination at the scene carried out by pathologist Dr David Gee would give police confirmation.

The three top detectives involved in the hunt for the Ripper, Detective Superintendent Dick Holland, Detective Chief Superintendent Trevor Laplish, and Assisant Chief Constable George Oldfield, visited the scene of the killing the morning after. Their worst fears were confirmed.

Two days later, police confirmed they were now offering a reward of £25,000 for information leading to the arrest and conviction of the Yorkshire Ripper.

When, three months after the Ripper's latest murder, George Oldfield released details of the audio tape sent to him by Wearside Jack, more than 1,300 telephone calls were made to police in Halifax alone from people who believed they knew who he was or had heard the voice before.

Four days after broadcasting the tape, police released excerpts from the third letter they had received from Wearside Jack. The letter was received by George Oldfield almost two weeks before the murder of Josephine Whitaker in the Halifax park. As he did in the tape, Wearside Jack taunted police in his latest letter.

But police believed his reference in the letter to the next time he was "up north" was a simple attempt by Jack to fool them into believing he lived south of Yorkshire. Mr Oldfield told the Yorkshire Post: "I believe he lives and works amongst us here in West Yorkshire. He definitely originates from the North East but I feel he is down here. I believe this letter is genuine and I hope people will study the handwriting carefully to see if they have ever seen it before."

On the same day that police in West Yorkshire released details of the "up north" letter, police in the North East had swooped on a small end-terraced house in Darlington, County Durham, after a tip-off from a neighbour. The neighbour had found newspaper cuttings of the Yorkshire Ripper killings, a number of medical books, microscopes and earphones while she was searching for a lost child at the house in Albert Street in the North Road area of the market town.

After examining the papers and other items, police were of the opinion they had been collected by a student who had probably been preparing a thesis. No suspicion fell on the student who had occupied the house and he was not linked in any way to the hoax letters and tape that had been sent to police. The materials had been discovered by the neighbour two weeks previously but she only alerted police after hearing the "I'm Jack" tape.

In the tape, Jack told police he may strike again in September, 1979. The Ripper did strike again that month, on September 2, killing what was believed to be his 12th victim. The mutilated body of student Barbara Leach was discovered in the back yard of a house in Bradford. "Ripper Keeps His Promise", was the headline the following day in the Sunderland Echo. The Yorkshire

Post reported that police "feared he had carried out a bizarre promise in a taped message delivered to police to kill again in September".

The murder of Barbara Leach intensified the hunt for the Yorkshire Ripper, both in West Yorkshire and in Sunderland. There were hundreds of police officers now working on the case and thousands of lines of inquiry were being followed up day and night. It was hoped that the net was closing in on Wearside Jack.

Within days of the death of Barbara Leach, hundreds more calls were received by police. At least a further 200 calls were made to the incident room in Sunderland's Gill Bridge Avenue Police Station.

Excerpts from the tape were broadcast again after the murder and the calls kept coming in. By October 1979, 22,000 statements had been taken by police, a total of 200,000 people had been interviewed or at least questioned, the police had visited 25,000 homes and they had checked 172,000 vehicles. Northumbria Police had set up its own budget specifically for the Ripper inquiry. The "Dial the Ripper" telephone line was still open.

The day before Barbara Leach was murdered, Sunderland had played Oldham away at Oldham and, as usual, thousands of Sunderland fans had travelled to see the match. Police worked on the theory that Wearside Jack may have been among the crowd at the match, but the line of inquiry drew a blank.

Then, in the Yorkshire Ripper's stalking ground, all went quiet for 12 months.

Behind the scenes, police were working flat out trying to catch Wearside Jack, alias the Yorkshire Ripper. No potential suspect would slip through the net. After almost a year had passed, senior officers began believing the Ripper's reign of terror had come to an end. But he struck again in Farsley, in August, 1980, killing 47-year-old Marguerite Walls. And three months later he killed a 20-year-old student in Leeds.

On the day of the Ripper's killing of the Leeds student - November 17 - the question on thousands of television soap fans' lips was "Who shot J.R. Ewing". That night J.R., in the popular American soap *Dallas* had been shot by an unknown assailant.

As hundreds of people in Leeds were glued to their television sets, Miss Jacqueline Hill, a student of French, was walking at the rear of the Arndale Centre, a shopping centre in Headingley, almost in view of her home at the students' halls of residence.

Miss Hill's parents, who lived near Middlesbrough, had read about the Ripper murders in West Yorkshire and they were so concerned about their daughter's safety, that they had persuaded her to move from her lodgings on the outskirts of Leeds into the halls of residence.

On the night she was attacked, Miss Hill, who was also a Sunday school teacher and hoped to become a probation officer, had attended a seminar in Leeds city centre on the subject of the probation service. She was on her way to the students' halls of residence and had only got off the bus minutes before she was attacked.

Ripper squad detectives were immediately called in and a pathologist carried out a post mortem examination on the body of Miss Hill, who had suffered extensive head injuries. Initially police found no evidence to link her murder with the Ripper, who last struck four months earlier in Farsley and almost a year before that in Bradford.

One early theory was that the attack on Miss Hill could be linked to a similar attack on a young woman in Headingley two months before. Inquiries later revealed that Miss Hill was, indeed, attacked by the Yorkshire Ripper. She was his 13th - and what turned out to be his last - victim.

After the attack on Miss Hill, West Yorkshire detectives, who were liaising closely with their counterparts in the Northumbria force, visited houses in Leeds where men from Sunderland were known to be living or lodging. "There has been close liaison with Northumbria Police," said a police spokesman.

With the Ripper's murder toll standing at 13, the pressure on police to catch him became more intense than ever. The biggest manhunt ever carried out by police in Britain was hotting up. No expense would be spared.

Police in West Yorkshire liaised ever more closely with police in Sunderland. A team of at least 50 civil servants was drafted into Leeds, occupying a number of offices, one of them near the city's main railway station, and in Sunderland's civic centre a team of detectives worked closely with staff in the registrar's department, checking and double checking the names, ages and addresses of potential suspects.

The hunt for Wearside Jack had reached its peak. And nowhere in the country was police activity more obvious than in Sunderland and, in particular, in the former pit village of Castletown in the north of Sunderland, where, it was believed, Wearside Jack was born and possibly still lived.

The Chief Constable of West Yorkshire, Ronald Gregory (pictured left) and his Assistant Chief Constable George Oldfield, were coming under increasing and intense pressure in the hunt for Wearside Jack/The Yorkshire Ripper. Picture: *The Sunderland Echo.*

CHAPTER THREE

Gill Bridge

A copy of the cassette tape made by Wearside Jack was brought by police from West Yorkshire to an incident room at Sunderland's Gill Bridge Police Station in the town centre several days, if not weeks, before it was broadcast to the public. The central police station, next door to Sunderland Magistrates' Court, was always the base for any major inquiry in Sunderland.

The inquiry was going on at a time long before police forces across the country started using hi-tech equipment such as computers and databases and years before the major advances in forensic science and other investigative techniques.

Sunderland's Gill Bridge Police Station had one of the division's only portable tape cassette recorders, in the hands of Scenes of Crimes Officer John Yearnshire, and he was one of the first police officers in Sunderland to hear the voice of Wearside Jack. Later, he made copies of the tape to be given to police officers making door-to-door inquiries.

Mr Yearnshire, now retired, says: "We had the only portable audio equipment in the building. When we got the tape, some officers got together to listen to it and some thought the dialect of the man was pitmatic.

"There was one particular officer, Inspector Alan Davidson, who had been brought up in Castletown, and he firmly believed the man had a Castletown accent. There were one or two other police officers from that area who were asked to listen to it and they formed the same opinion.

"To me, the voice did sound local. It was definitely a North East accent but, as I'm not originally from Sunderland, I wasn't able to be more specific. Whoever the man was, he seemed to be well informed about the murders."

Mr Yearnshire and his small team were also responsible for examining anonymous letters that were sent to police from people who believed they knew Wearside Jack. Mr Yearnshire says: "There were quite a few anonymous letters which had to be forensically examined.

"We needed to go through all the usual procedures just in case the named person was the man we were looking for. A lot of people wrote in to say it sounded exactly like someone they knew. The letters we received were all anonymous but each one had to be followed up properly. Nothing ever came of them."

A copy of the tape was sent to the Technical Support division for police in the North East at the Durham Police headquarters at Aykley Heads from where more copies were made for distribution to frontline officers whose job it was to try to track down Wearside Jack.

A linguistics expert, Professor Stanley Ellis, from the University of Leeds, had analysed the voice and came to the same conclusion as Inspector Alan Davidson: That the voice on the tape was that of a man who came from the former pit village of Castletown. Professor Ellis spent some time in the village recording a range of local men's voices.

Professor Ellis was convinced of the Castletown connection. This year, Prof Ellis said he did not wish to make any further comment on his research as it had "hung round his neck like an albatross" for 20 years.

In the incident room at Gill Bridge thousands of card indexes were soon building up in the paper-based inquiry, containing the names, ages, and addresses of all the men police had to eliminate for the massive inquiry. The scale of the inquiry could be measured by the number of card indexes in the "carousel" used by police. At the end of the inquiry it contained about 9,000 cards.

One of the officers manning the incident room was Detective Constable Charlie Russell. The officer, now retired, says: "At the time I worked in the information gathering room at Gill Bridge. I know that the voice expert did many inquiries across the North East. He went around visiting pubs, clubs and shops just listening to how people spoke.

"Before the tape was released to the public, I was working in the west of Sunderland and me and other officers were asked to listen to it and give our own interpretation of where the speaker might be from.

"Personally, I initially thought it was a voice from out in the sticks, County Durham, you know, perhaps the Willington or Crook areas. But now, of course, I know I was wrong."

Mr Russell adds: "The people working in the information room were a mixture of detectives and uniform. In the room we collated information that came in from the public. There was an overwhelming response after the tape was broadcast. We also went out regularly looking for information.

"We were back and forwards all the time with documents containing a lot of information. We soon had thousands of cards and documents.

"It was the first time I had come across a carousel, which was basically a big metal base with a rod leading to an upturned metal dish on the top where all the cards were stored. The cards, all about three inches by five inches, were in alphabetical order and contained the names, date of birth, occupation and addresses of everyone interviewed, the time and date of the interview and the name of the investigating officer.

"You could spin this dish and get to the card you were looking for quite easily. But it was time consuming and now, of course, everything is computerised.

"As the inquiry progressed the first dish - and it could hold about 5,000 cards - was filled and we had to put a second on the top. That, too, soon became about 80 per cent full. So we had, in those two dishes and within a few months, about 9,000 cards, all of which were indexed."

Mr Russell had information on the man police were hunting. He says: "West Yorkshire Police had sat on the tape for a few days or weeks before it was released to the general public. One of the women the Ripper was said to have murdered, he was supposed to have bitten into one of her breasts. That's why we were asked to look for a man with a distinctive gap in his front teeth.

"During the inquiry, every scrap of information was followed up. But it turned out that if that fella was the Ripper he appeared to hold no secrets, because it was said that every bit of information in the letters and the tape could have been picked up from reports in the media."

Every scrap of information was, indeed, followed up but detectives in Sunderland did come across some obstacles. A senior officer in Sunderland wanted to get information on local people through the Department of Health and Social Security at the massive national complex in Longbenton, North Tyneside. The complex, which opened on July 5, 1948, houses the national insurance numbers of every British citizen wherever they are in the world. At the time of the Wearside Jack/Ripper inquiry the earnings-related pension scheme was still in existence and the centre received millions of pieces of information in batches over six-week periods.

The information databases at Longbenton could prove to be an invaluable investigative tool for officers working on the Ripper inquiry. But with civil liberties and personal privacy becoming more of an issue in the late 1970s permission to obtain information from the centre proved difficult.

One Sunderland officer who worked on the case remembers the problems detectives encountered. The former detective, who wants to remain anonymous, says: "From all the evidence at the scene of the murders it was believed the Ripper was in some way connected with engineering.

"We wanted to interview men working in engineering locally but what was needed was their national insurance numbers. The Department of Health and Social Security at Longbenton, North Tyneside, was asked to provide these national insurance numbers but we got a big no, no.

"All I can think is that, at the time, unions were still very strong and left wing and they must have thought it would infringe on civil liberties. What happened then was that police had to apply to the Home Secretary of the time to order the DHSS to give us access to the information. Once permission was given, the DHSS did everything they could to help police."

During the inquiry, police had focused their attentions on employees at the David Brown gear factory on Sunderland's Pallion Industrial Estate. David Brown's head office was in Huddersfield and the men employed at Pallion fitted the offender profile of the Ripper in two ways: They were involved in some kind of engineering and would have had reason to travel to West Yorkshire from time to time. The movements of the men at the factory were checked by police but inquiries drew a blank.

Detectives in Sunderland decided to follow yet another line of inquiry. Speech experts in Scotland had listened to the "I'm Jack" tape and had concluded that the man, as well as coming from Sunderland, had at least one, and possibly two, speech impediments.

Police worked on the theory that Jack, at some stage in his life, had some kind of speech therapy. They set about trying to discover his identity by checking the records of all the registered speech therapists across the North East of England. Again, police came across an obstacle and, unlike the earlier barrier placed in their way by the DHSS, this one could not be moved.

Despite the massive police inquiry and the fact that Wearside Jack was believed to have murdered so many women, the speech therapists decided that client confidentiality was paramount. Police never got to check the records of their clients, despite their persuasive efforts, because permission to do so was refused.

As police in West Yorkshire and in Sunderland continued their inquiries a team of at least 50 civil servants was drafted into Leeds to help police. The civil servants were employed by the Department of Health and Social Security, the Department of Employment, the Inland Revenue and the Ministry of Defence, among others. All possessed important information on members of the public and members of the Armed forces, information that could prove relevant to the inquiry.

The extent of the involvement of the Civil Service in the Ripper inquiry was never made public, as all the civil servants involved had signed the Official Secrets Act and, for the purposes of the

Ripper inquiry, their involvement was an "official secret". Disclosure of any information would have led to instant dismissal.

One civil servant, who, for obvious reasons cannot be named, remembers the inquiry well. He says: "I remember that our involvement in the inquiry had some sort of covert codename, it was either Operation Pullover or Operation Cardigan.

"All the civil servants were working at a number of bases. There was one base on the third or fourth floor of an office block directly opposite Leeds main railway station, one in Gipton Place in Leeds, and another on the outskirts of the city in Guiseley.

"I interviewed three or four suspects in a Civil Service setting and a police officer and a psychologist would pose as civil servants themselves, watching for the man's body language or other tell-tale signs.

"One man I interviewed was a fairly well-known pervert, another was an engineer and another was known to travel quite frequently from the North East to West Yorkshire where he had relatives. One fitted the description but none, of course, turned out to be the Ripper or the man who sent the tape.

"The police had drawn up a 50-suspect queue and they would concentrate their inquiries on those 50 people, eliminating some when they had been checked out and then including other suspects higher up on the list.

"There was a kind of psychological profile drawn up of the man they were hunting. He was said to be about 5ft 8ins, a loner who probably lived with his mother, who worked in engineering and was probably a pervert or a repressed homosexual.

"He was thought to be about 5ft 8ins because some of the hammer blows were struck upwards and one of the victims was said to be quite tall. If I recollect correctly the man was also supposed to be left handed."

The civil servant adds: "The suspects would be called into a tax office or an employment office or whatever and be interviewed by one of the civil servants with the police officer and the psychologist present. The thinking behind it was that if the man was interviewed at a police station he may be on his guard but if interviewed in a different setting he may still be on his guard, but for different reasons.

"There was a large number of civil servants working on this inquiry at the time; I think at least 50. We had a number of meetings with police officers and I remember meeting a consultant forensic psychiatrist at the Highroyd Hospital in Leeds.

"He told me there had been a special unit set up in the hospital for when the Ripper was caught. He said it had a bedroom, a sitting room and a bathroom, where all the plumbing was in-built. When the Ripper was caught he was to be placed in that room and kept under constant surveillance. The psychiatrist was quite a chilling character, I remember, but he spoke in such a matter-of-fact way."

The civil servant, along with his colleagues who worked with him at the time, were to discover that all their efforts had been pointless. Now, 20 years after the inquiry, he still feels there are questions that need answers. He says: "There's still quite a few unanswered questions. Was the hoaxer the killer of the girl from Preston? Was he working with the Ripper? Who was Wearside Jack and why did he send the tape? There was a hell of a lot of work went into that inquiry, but it all came to nothing."

Sunderland's Gill Bridge Police Station, where a major incident room was set up in the hunt for the Yorkshire Ripper/Wearside Jack. After a few months there were about 9,000 card indexes in the incident room, containing the personal details of men who had to be eliminated from the inquiry. Picture: *The Sunderland Echo.*

CHAPTER FOUR

THE STOCK POT

In the 20 years from 1979 up to 1999 in the Sunderland area command of the Northumbria Police force there were few unsolved major crimes. As police in the city geared up for the Millennium they were proud of their track record in solving serious crimes such as murder and rape.

A killer known as the Sunderland Strangler, Steven Grieveson, was behind bars for the murder of three Sunderland teenagers as a result of one of the biggest murder inquiries in the division during the two decades. Serial rapist Kevin Lakeman, originally charged with more than a dozen rapes spanning a ten-year period, was also serving life behind bars.

Lakeman, who was caught because senior detectives were able to link him through DNA analysis with a particularly brutal rape in Sunderland city centre, terrorised women in the north of the city; on council housing estates such as Town End Farm, Red House and Downhill, on the border with South Tyneside.

A flat on the Downhill estate was the scene of one of Sunderland's still unsolved murders. Former stripper and known prostitute Julie Perigo was savagely attacked. Press appeals for information at the time of her killing and later on the anniversary dates of her murder failed to give police the vital lead they needed in tracking down her murderer.

Nearer the city centre, in the same stalking ground of the Sunderland Strangler, around Roker and Monkwearmouth, still on the north side of the River Wear, teenage runaway Simon Martin had been battered to death in a derelict house on the Roker seafront. The house, Gillside House, was a known haunt for local glue sniffers. His murder remains unsolved.

A third unsolved murder, that of seven-year-old Nikki Allan, who lived in Wear Garth in the city's East End, was still on the files of detectives in Sunderland. A local man was charged with her murder after she was stabbed 37 times and battered to death and left in a derelict building in High Street West, not far from her home. The man charged was found not guilty after a six-week trial in Leeds.

The uniformed police superintendent in the Sunderland area command at the time of Nikki's murder was Superintendent Alex Price, a respected police officer, with detailed local knowledge and a straightforward, common-sense approach. Supt Price liaised closely with other officers in the murder case and with Nikki's family. He also sat at Press conferences, updating the media at every stage of the inquiry.

Fifteen years earlier Alex Price was a uniformed sergeant working on another still unsolved crime; the hunt for Wearside Jack. He was in charge of ten uniformed police constables in the north of Sunderland who formed what was known as the Special Patrol Group. His team, along with detectives, was at the forefront of the inquiry to find the man who sent the hoax tape and letters, and officers concentrated their in-depth inquiries in the area in and around Castletown, Hylton Castle, Red House, Downhill and Town End Farm.

Up until near the end of October, 1979, Sergeant Price and his team were working out of a caravan which toured the estates. Nearing the end of the month the "Ripper Squad", as it became known, moved into a former police house in Bexhill Road, Town End Farm.

The reason for the move was the number of files built up since the massive public appeal for help in tracking down Wearside Jack only three months earlier. Detective Inspector Dave Zackrisson said: "The amount of administration built up during the inquiry had become so large that we needed a larger and more permanent building in the area."

Alex Price, now retired but still living in Sunderland, had been stationed in the west of the town before he moved over to the SPG in 1979. He was with the Special Patrol Group for two years, but his work was not confined to the Ripper inquiry.

Alex Price, as a police superintendent, when he headed Press conferences for the Nikki Allan murder inquiry in Sunderland. Picture: *The Sunderland Echo.*

Mr Price remembers the inquiry well. He says: "The tape itself was quite haunting. Every time I hear that song by Andrew Gold *'Thank you for being a Friend'* I always think of Peter Sutcliffe. It was so unusual for a murderer to go so far and be so blase about it. I am sure the West Yorkshire Police had their doubts, but they were struggling.

"Anyway, the inquiry had to be bottomed out and we couldn't allow ourselves to think we were wasting our time. There was a job to be done and we had to be professional about it. It was a major inquiry.

"The Special Patrol Group had been taken away from normal duties and a major incident room was set up at Gill Bridge Avenue Police Station, which was staffed mainly by CID officers.

"It was a typical set up for a big inquiry and it was set up as a direct result of the tape. There were ten CID officers working in the Gill Bridge incident room and there were ten uniformed officers, under my control, based at the old police house in Town End Farm."

The former senior officer adds: "To complement the work carried out at the old police house and at Gill Bridge we were also still using the caravan to tour the estates and we would try to catch people as they passed.

"We were looking for males, aged 20 to 40, who could drive and had reason to travel down to West Yorkshire. Because of the scientific evidence we were also looking for someone with an eighth-of-an-inch gap in his top two front teeth.

"Because of the severity of the attacks members of the public were only too happy to help us. After they had heard the tape everyone was saying the Ripper was a Wearsider. Personally I always found the voice on the tape to be a little manufactured. I didn't think the voice was particularly natural but it was obviously North Eastern and probably Wearside.

"When it was released it was electrifying and we always had to keep in our minds that the Ripper could be a Wearsider. Whoever did send it was obviously a callous individual."

Sgt Price and his team soon discovered that anyone who had the slightest inkling that they knew Wearside Jack, would inform the police. Local women, in particular, were keen to put names forward - even if it was the name of their own son, boyfriend, or husband.

Mr Price says: "Many thousands of names were put forward and all had to be investigated. Thousands of men were interviewed.

"When we were carrying out door-to-door inquiries we had to bear in mind we could be attacked at any time. For that reason we would always double up - in other words all door-to-door inquiries were always carried out by two police officers. Every police officer on that inquiry was given a blown-up extract from one of the letters, a copy of the tape and a portable cassette player

"To support our inquiries I and other officers went for regular briefings in West Yorkshire with other officers, including George Oldfield. Likewise, some West Yorkshire officers would travel to Wearside for briefings as well. I saw videos and photographs of the murder scenes. It was really quite horrific."

As well as the travelling by Sunderland officers to West Yorkshire and vice-versa, a team of senior detectives from West Yorskhire was permanently based in Sunderland during the inquiry, staying at the expensive Roker Hotel on the seafront - one of the more up-market hotels in the town.

No expense appeared to have been spared. But there were other, unexpected, expenses coming out of both forces' often over-stretched budgets. One was a quite hefty bill from the Roker Hotel - not for board and lodging but for damages.

An officer who worked on the case remembers the reason for the extra charges.

He says: "The story was that one of the senior officers had turned on the taps to run a bath unaware that the water had been switched off. There was a telephone call for him at the hotel and he went to answer, forgetting that the taps had been left on.

"Later on, the bath overflowed and the weight of the water made the ceiling in the room below collapse. There was quite a bit of damage, not just to the ceiling but the carpets and other furnishings as well. Some of the Sunderland officers thought it was quite funny at the time. I'm almost sure it was West Yorkshire who had to foot the bill."

During the intense, and often boring, routine police work during the inquiry, there were lighter moments. Police officers, both uniformed and CID, were asking the same questions, of similar people, in the same area, day in, day out. Job gossip and jokes about some of the more unusual aspects of the inquiry provided a little light relief and reinforced the already-strong sense of camaraderie in the Ripper Squad.

At the north Sunderland base in Bexhill Road, Town End Farm, senior officers decided to make full use of the four-ring electric cooker in the kitchen. If an army marches on its stomach it was decided the Ripper Squad would at least pound the beat with enough food in its belly to keep it going during the long inquiry.

One of the squad's detectives - who shall remain nameless - "borrowed" a massive cooking pot which was so big it took up all four rings on the cooker. It came from the kitchens of either the force headquarters at Ponteland or the Queen Elizabeth Hospital in Gateshead. It was to provide police officers with their lunch, dinner and even, at times, their breakfast.

One detective recalls what became known as the "stock pot". He says: "It was bloody massive, and it was very welcome during the winter months. One of the detectives brought this tin cooking pot, put it on the stove, and told everyone he was going to make some stew.

"The officers on house-to-house inquiries would call into the local fruit and veg shops and the butchers and they were given scraps of meat and loads of veg. All this was put into the pot for stew. The pot was there for ages because more would be added to it every day. It was hardly ever emptied and cleaned. There was a big ladle in it and anyone who was peckish would just help themselves."

Another officer, a beat bobby who was a member of the Special Patrol Group, used an unmarked Ford Escort van to travel to outlying areas, such as County Durham or Newcastle, to interview "Wearside Jack" suspects who had moved out of the area. He worked nine to five, Monday to Friday but, he recalls, the van would never be available on a Friday morning.

"That's because the van was used by a couple of CID to go to the market at the Team Valley in Gateshead and stock up on food," he says. "They would come back with loads of meat and vegetables.

"We each paid 50p a week towards the stock pot. During the winter months it was welcome but the stew was always on, even during the summer, and we ended up sweating buckets. The dumplings; I had never seen dumplings as big before and I haven't seen any bigger than that since. They were like footballs!"

After several months knocking on doors, interviewing local people, checking their details, movements, descriptions, and cross-referencing every bit of information with the card indexes at the Gill Bridge incident room, and double-checking that the interviewee could be eliminated from the inquiry, the first team from the Special Patrol Group had really had enough.

Detective Constable Ian Martin (left) and Detective Sergeant Ged Duffy, of the Sunderland Ripper Squad, outside the squad's base in Bexhill Road, Town End Farm. Picture: *The Sunderland Echo.*

A second team of SPG officers was drafted into the Town End Farm base. And, by November, 1979, the pressure to catch the Yorkshire Ripper/Wearside Jack had become so intense a "fresh pair of eyes" was appointed to spearhead the overall joint inquiry.

Commander Jim Neville, from Scotland Yard, and his right-hand man Detective Chief Inspector Jim Bolton, arrived in West Yorkshire on November 21 and visited Sunderland later that month before preparing a report on the progress of the inquiry for West Yorkshire's Chief Constable Ronald Gregory.

Questions were already being asked: Were police right to place so much credence on the authenticity of the "Wearside Jack" tape? Could it be a hoaxer? Had something which could help police catch the Ripper/Jack been overlooked? The massive police inquiry had already cost taxpayers millions of pounds.

In Town End Farm, Sunderland, the new SPG team was settling in and getting used to its surroundings - and the stock pot. One of the officers recalls the tedious nature of the inquiry. He says: "We were the second SPG team to go in. Basically the work was so laborious the first team had got sick of it.

"Like the first team, we were assigned specific actions or tasks to locate people and eliminate them from the inquiry. We would always pair up and we were expected to complete at least two actions every day. We worked a five-day week, Monday to Friday, 9am until 5pm. There was only ever a little overtime worked.

"We knew the man we were looking for had links with Castletown and that he was also a B secretor. That was why we were always asking people for saliva samples. Our packs were full of sample tubes.

"We also had pro-formas which contained four sheets. They were about half the size of an A4 sheet of paper. We also had copies of letters that we would dictate to the men and they would have to write down what we said. It was basically like asking them to write to someone.

"These letters were put together from the originals but they weren't verbatim copies. They contained certain words or phrases which were unusual but specific to the original letters, such as two certain words used together or words that figured heavily in the letters. I remember there was a certain way the writer formed the letter G, and that was something we would always look out for.

"If , when we got actions, it was found that the person we were looking for had moved from the address, say in Red House or Town End Farm, that information would go back to the Bexhill Road base and then on to the Civic Centre. It would be checked again and then it would come back to us."

The massive police inquiry to find the Yorkshire Ripper/Wearside Jack was now, as ever, intense. Police in Sunderland and in West Yorkshire were still working on the premise that the Ripper and Jack were one and the same. Although doubts had been raised about the tape's authenticity they were never taken seriously enough to stop or even scale down the inquiry in Sunderland in favour of other leads.

The real Ripper killed what was thought to be his 11th victim in September, 1979, his 12th victim in August, 1980, and his 13th in November, 1980. By that time he had already been interviewed by police - several times - and eliminated from their inquiries. There was one thing immediately recognisable about Peter William Sutcliffe: He did not speak with a Wearside accent. As one police officer now comments: "You did not have to be Sherlock Holmes to work that one out."

As for Wearside Jack, he remained at large right up until the end of 1980 and remains free still, as Sutcliffe languishes in a "special" hospital cell in Broadmoor. An officer who tried to track down Wearside Jack says: "Whoever he was, he has done bloody well to keep it quiet all these years. He could be still living in Sunderland or he could be dead."

CONFIDENTIAL—For Police use only.

WEST YORKSHIRE METROPOLITAN POLICE

Friday, 20th JULY, 1979

MURDER OF WOMEN IN YORKSHIRE, LANCASHIRE AND GREATER MANCHESTER

In furtherance of the enquiries being made in connection with the above cases, all Police Officers handling correspondence received from members of the public are asked to compare the handwriting with that reproduced below. Likewise, all Operational Officers dealing with male members of the public between the ages of 25 and 55 years who have a North East accent should carefully examine any handwriting obtained from that person. In all cases where there is any apparent similarity, photo copies of the handwriting and details of the source from which obtained, should be passed to the Incident Room at Halifax.

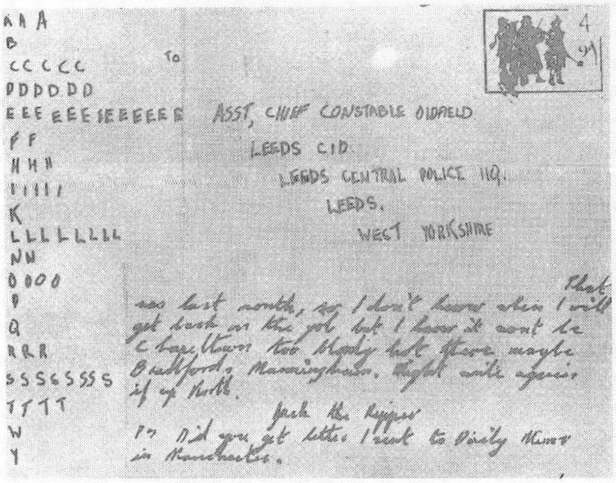

The capital letters reproduced in the margin represent particular identifiable features.

If copies of the tape recorded message are not readily available at Police Stations, the voice can be heard by dialling Leeds 469111 (STD code 0532).

As this confidential police document shows, detectives interviewing suspects in the Ripper/Wearside Jack inquiry and those detectives looking at thousands of items of post at the main post office in West Sunniside, Sunderland, were particularly interested in how the writer formed certain letters. The hoax letters had been analysed by a handwriting expert. Those letters would feature heavily in the script that detectives would dictate to suspects for them to provide a sample of their handwriting. One form of words in the script dictated was: "How's your Elsie?"

WEST YORKSHIRE METROPOLITAN POLICE

CRIMINAL INTELLIGENCE

Western Operational Area, Bradford

Tel. Bradford 23422

30th May, 1977

CONFIDENTIAL — FOR POLICE USE ONLY

PROSTITUTE MURDERS

1. At 9.30 p.m. on either a Wednesday or Friday during March, 1975, **Barbara Kathryn Jennie Miller,** born 12.2.41, an active prostitute in the Wolverhampton, Derby, and Manningham area of Bradford, picked up the after-described client in a public house in Lumb Lane, Bradford, and she was taken to a quarry in the Bolton Woods district of Bradford in a vehicle she describes as a **Land Rover,** hard top and fairly long. The vehicle is further described as being possibly blue with dirty cream top and in dirty condition, six-inch tear in black vinyl of passenger seat, with white coloured square petrol can and sacking behind driver's seat.

The man stopped the vehicle, went round the nearside, opened the passenger door and ordered the woman out. She refused and was pulled out of the vehicle, following which a violent struggle took place and she was punched in the stomach, chest and face. The woman eventually escaped, but did not report the matter to the police.

Her attacker is described as follows:—

Man, 35 - 40 years, 5ft. 8in., stocky build, untidy ginger hair, thin but not receding. Full ginger beard and moustache which was bushy on cheeks but cut short under chin, bushy ginger eyebrows, possibly blue eyes, yellow stained teeth, long nose, straight and turned up, ruddy complexion, possible Irish accent with slight Birmingham dialect, thick hands and fingers, plain gold square ring on little finger of right hand.

ON BACK OF LEFT HAND WAS A 3-4in. SCAR FROM THE KNUCKLE OF RING FINGER IN A CURVE TO OUTSIDE OF HAND. BLUE AND RED TATTOO ON BACK OF ONE FOREARM WHICH TAPERED TO A POINT BELOW CUFF.

Wearing well-worn dark grey plain jacket, dirty white shirt, narrow black tie, blue overalls in a dirty condition, bib and brace fastening, torn at knee revealing trousers similar to jacket, rubber lace-up boots.

2. At 7.35 a.m. 30th October, 1975, the body of **Wilma McCann,** born 1.7.47, was found in playing fields off Scott Hall Road, Leeds 7.

Continued overleaf.

This confidential police report - one of two pages - was produced in May, 1977, almost a year before the first two hoax letters were posted by Wearside Jack and almost two years before the tape was posted in Sunderland. It reveals how detectives believed the Ripper was driving around killing or attempting to kill women, in a Land Rover or Jeep-type vehicle. It also shows one of the first photo-fits of the suspected serial killer.

— 2 —

3. At 8.05 a.m. 21st January, 1976, the body of **Emily Monica Jackson,** 42 years, an active prostitute in the Chapeltown district of Leeds, was found in a derelict building in Manor Street, Leeds 7.

The assailant is believed to have been wearing heavy-ribbed rubber boots or heavy Wellington boots.

It is desired to trace the after-described who was seen to pick up the deceased shortly before 7 p.m. 20th January in a **Land Rover,** outside the Gaiety public house, Gaythorne Terrace, Leeds 7.

Man, about 50 years, fat build, mousy coloured hair, ear-length, full beard (unshaped), ginger/blond coloured sideburns same colour as beard, eyebrows, sideburns and beard very bushy, round nose which appeared squashed, eyes closed giving appearance he was going to sleep, face may be scarred.

LEFT HAND DEFORMED, WITH DISTINCTIVE SCAR, AS IF IT HAD BEEN BURNED, EXTENDING FROM KNUCKLES ON THE BACK OF THE HAND TO THE WRIST, NORMAL SKIN COLOUR BUT STRETCHED AND WRINKLED.

Believed wearing plain gold square-topped ring on third finger left hand, also plain gold ring second finger left hand. Wearing dark blue working jacket, believed anorak type, dark blue overall-type trousers, black footwear, possibly boots or Wellingtons with thick sole pattern.

His clothing was dusty and he appeared to have come from work on a building site.

The **Land Rover,** green colour, had a hard top which was darker than the rest of the body, passenger door appeared to have been patched up with grey/silver paint, appeared as if door had been scraped, normal driver and passenger windows, with small aerial on front nearside wing near windscreen, bench seat.

Attention is drawn to the similarity of the driver of the **Land Rover** and that of the man involved in the incident at Bradford in March, 1975, but due to the lapse of time the suspect may not now wear a beard or be in possession of the vehicle described.

It is also desired to trace the after-described who has associated with prostitutes in the Chapeltown area of Leeds and who is believed to have been an associate of **Jackson.** He has previously picked up prostitutes, taken them to an isolated area and assaulted them.

Man, labourer or motor mechanic, born 41-46 years, 5ft. 6in., proportionate build, short grey hair, thin moustache, small ears, Irish accent. Wearing dark grey overcoat, white shirt, coloured tie, dirty blue cardigan with two square pockets, dark grey trousers with brown leather belt, brown slip-on shoes, red underpants.

In possession of dark grey coloured jeep-type vehicle in dilapidated condition (believed **Land Rover**). In the back were sacks and three tins of oil (the small type used by motorists). There were also a number of tools.

4. At 7.50 a.m. Sunday, 6th February, 1977, the body of **Irene Richardson,** born 28.3.48, was found at the rear of the Sports Changing Rooms, Soldiers Field, Roundhay, Leeds.

Tyre marks found at the scene indicate that a medium-size saloon or van may have been used in the commission of the offence. Two of the tyres are well-worn India Autoway make. The other tyres are Esso E.110 and Pneumant. All are of the cross-ply type. The size of tyre could **not** be fitted to a **Land Rover.**

5. At 6.30 p.m., Sunday, 24th April, 1977, the body of **Patricia Atkinson,** born 9.5.44, an active prostitute in the Manningham area of Bradford, was found in her flat at Bradford.

The deceased left a public house in Bradford at 10.15 p.m., 23rd April, and at that time was apparently under the influence of alcohol.

Printed and Published at Police Headquarters, Wakefield

This second page from the confidential police report, reveals how tyre marks at the scene of one of the Ripper murders, that of Irene Richardson, proved the killer could not have been driving a Land Rover or Jeep-type vehicle. From the tyre marks, the vehicle's wheel-base was discovered, and police knew they were looking for the driver of a Ford Corsair, an Austin Cambridge or a Morris Oxford. Sutcliffe drove a Ford Corsair. But Sunderland men driving any of the three makes of car needed to be eliminated from the inquiry.

CHAPTER FIVE

A Shadow over the Village

Castletown is one of those areas described as a village but which looks nothing like a village at all. It has its workingmen's club, a few local pubs, a row of shops and a local sports centre. It doesn't have its own library and lacks many of the facilities in the council house areas that sprung up around it, such as the Downhill estate, Red House, Town End Farm and Hylton Castle.

But, like other areas of Sunderland such as Silksworth, Castletown grew up around the local pit, Hylton Colliery. It was a pit village and is still referred to as a village, even though Hylton Colliery closed in the mid 1970s and Sunderland's last remaining pit, Wearmouth Colliery, suffered the same fate in the early 1990s.

There was once a railway line which served the local pits and the shipyards. That line became the A1231 Wessington Way, one of the main routes in and out of the north of Sunderland. On the site of the old colliery now stands a McDonald's drive-thru restaurant, a furniture store and a cash and carry.

For strangers driving into north Sunderland the village could be missed with a blink of the eye. Outside Sunderland, Castletown is probably little-known, but it does have two well-known sporting sons; Mickey Gray, a left winger with Sunderland Football Club and Billy Hardy, who has held the British, European and Commonwealth boxing titles at featherweight and bantamweight.

The village was also the home of the MP for Sunderland North, Bill Etherington, a former pitman. He, along with thousands of other men who lived or were born in Castletown, were questioned by police in an inquiry which put the village on the national television news and attracted reporters and photographers in their droves - the hunt for Wearside Jack.

Linda Nicholson has lived in the same house in Castletown for 33 years, and remembers the impact the police and media activity had on the residents, and the chilling thought that there was a serial killer in their midst.

Her husband, Bob, a miner who worked at both Hylton Colliery and Wearmouth Colliery, who died before the Ripper inquiry, wrote news and cricket reports for the Sunderland Echo and, after his death, Mrs Nicholson took over writing the reports and became the village's correspondent for the Sunderland Echo's weekly supplement Neighbourhood News.

She says: "We didn't trust anybody really. The police came and asked us to shop anyone we knew who motored over the Pennines. I didn't know anyone who did that at the time.

"At the time, because they said the man who sent the tape came from Castletown, there was a lot of police activity in the village and there was a lot of interest in the village from the newspapers.

"There was one particular national newspaper report which made me angry. It just portrayed people in Castletown, typically, as all wearing cloth caps or working down the pits. It was awful. To me it had never been like that. It was always a nice village. Mind you, it's twice the size now what it was then because lots of houses have been built in the area."

Mrs Nicholson adds: "When I heard the tape and heard that the man was from Castletown I just couldn't believe it. I didn't think anyone in the village could do something like that. It was the same every time I heard it.

"The police came to every house in the village where there was a male living, including mine. Although my husband was dead, my son still lived at home. Everyone said the voice on the tape sounded familiar. The thing is, if he was from Castletown, he could still be alive now and still living in the village. I think that's frightening.

Coun Les Mann

"I thought I knew the voice but a lot of people thought the same. It was a shame because it made everyone suspicious of everyone else. The women were frightened to go out at night."

The media reports were, generally, all right, says local Labour councillor Les Mann, but some reports did anger local people in the way men in the village were portrayed as the stereotypical Northerner, interested in beer, whippets, and cigarettes.

Coun Mann says: "The papers were full of rubbish about Castletown. One national report said none of the men in Castletown owned a suit and went to work in their jumpers. That particular report incensed a lot of people and quite a few wrote to the editor to complain. It degraded the people of Castletown."

One member of the Sunderland Ripper Squad, Detective Constable George Virtue, found himself in the national media spotlight almost overnight. At the time the Northumbria Police Force did not have a dedicated Press and Public Relations Unit, as it does now, and Press inquiries were dealt with on the ground, often by rank-and-file officers.

Det Con Virtue, still a serving officer with Northumbria Police, based in Sunderland, found himself deluged with requests from television, radio and newspapers, national and local, for interviews, information and updates on how the inquiry was going.

He joined the police service in 1970 with Durham Constabulary and was posted to Sunderland, which - before the local government shake-up in 1974 - was then part of County Durham.
At the time of the Ripper/Wearside Jack inquiry he was with the North East Regional Crime Squad, then based in Newcastle. During his 29-year career with the police he spent his first five to six years with Sunderland CID at its base in Southwick, went up to the force headquarters in Ponteland for five years, to work on a job he cannot talk about, and then returned to Sunderland to work out of the city's Gill Bridge Avenue police station. It was quite unusual - and still is - for someone just signing up for a job in the police service to be given a post of Detective Constable.

Det Con George Virtue, pictured in May 1995, when he received a Chief Constable's commendation for bravery. Picture: *The Sunderland Echo*

Det Con Virtue says: "I was working with the Regional Crime Squad at the time and six officers were sent to work on the Ripper inquiry, three detective sergeants and three detective constables. We were posted from the RCS office in Newcastle to the incident room at Gill Bridge. I was on the inquiry for about ten months and one of my first jobs was setting up the caravan in Castletown."

The mobile caravan was the first base for Ripper Squad police in the north of Sunderland before they moved to the old police house in Town End Farm.

Det Con Virtue says: "I remember it was in Chiswick Square, Hylton Castle, for two to three months before it moved on. When I set the caravan up I was with the TSU (Territorial Support Unit) and I got them to fit a loudspeaker on it. I would play the tape over the loudspeakers on the hour, every hour.

"On one particular day there was a television crew and they wanted to film me walking about the streets. The tape recorder I had was huge, compared to what you can get these days. I got myself prepared for the film crew and walked up to a woman in the street, while the cameras were rolling, and I asked her if she had heard the tape.

"Her reply was blunt: 'I hear it every ****ing hour', she said - and remember this was supposed to be going out on live television. I don't think it did in the end. It turned out the woman lived in the same street where the caravan was, where the tape would be played on the loudspeakers every hour."

He adds: "At the time there wasn't a press office, as such, for Northumbria Police, and I seemed to be inundated with requests from the newspapers and television for interviews. I remember one girl reporter coming up and saying she wanted to see a workingmen's club, so I took her to the Red House Workingmen's Club.

"After I had finished with all the interviews I was sent down to the main post office in Sunderland, in West Sunniside. There was a team of four of us based there, working from 9am until 5pm every day, and, sometimes, there would be other officers working late-shift. The purpose was to track down who sent the letters.

"The bulk of the mail posted in Sunderland was coming through between about 6pm and 7pm. That's why we often worked late, or another team would be in the post office. Normally, I would be there around 8am for the first post to be sorted coming through. The teams at the post office were a mixture of detective constables and sergeants.

Detective Constable George Virtue talks to the head of Sunderland CID, Detective Superintendent Peter Docherty, inside the police caravan. Picture: *The Sunderland Echo*.

The envelopes which contained the taunting letters - and the tape - sent by Wearside Jack to the Assistant Chief Constable of West Yorkshire Police, George Oldfield, and to the Daily Mirror newspaper. The first was addressed to Mr Oldfield and postmarked March 8, 1978, the second was addressed to the Chief Editor at the Daily Mirror and was postmarked March 13, 1978. The third letter, forwarded to Mr Oldfield, was posted on March 23, 1979. The fourth envelope contained the tape and was also addressed to Mr Oldfield and posted in Sunderland in June, 1979. Picture: ***The Sunderland Echo.***

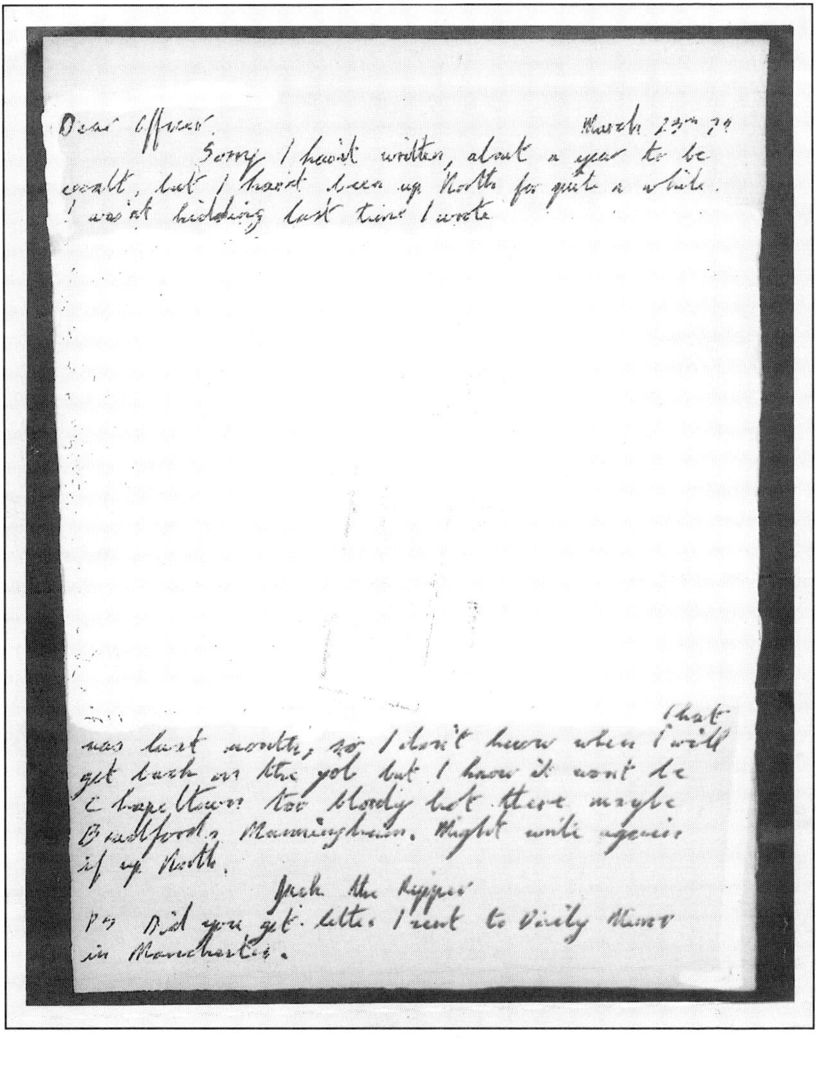

Dear Officer, March 23rd 79

Sorry I havn't written, about a year to be exact, but I hav'nt been up North for quite a while. I was'nt kidding last time I wrote

that was last month, so I don't know when I will get back on the job but I know it wont be Chapeltown too bloody hot there maybe Bradford's Manningham. Might write again if up North.

Jack the Ripper

PS Did you get letter I sent to Daily Mirror in Manchester.

The letter posted in Sunderland and dated March 23, 1979, contained information which police said could only be known by the killer. Extracts from the letter were made public in an effort to encourage people who recognised the handwriting to come forward. Certain words and phrases from this, and the other Wearside Jack letters, were used in a letter compiled by police which was dictated to hundreds of men on Wearside who were asked for samples of their handwriting. Picture: ***The Sunderland Echo.***

Detective Constable George Virtue, of the Sunderland Ripper squad, plays the Wearside Jack tape to local residents. The mobile caravan, which toured Castletown and Hylton Castle, can be seen top right in the picture. Picture: *Daily Mail.*

Hundreds of men in Castletown came under suspicion after linguistics expert Professor Stanley Ellis, of Leeds University, pinpointed the village as the likely area where Wearside Jack lived or grew up. Have you heard this voice before? asks Det Con Virtue as he plays the tape to a group of local men. Picture: *Daily Mail.*

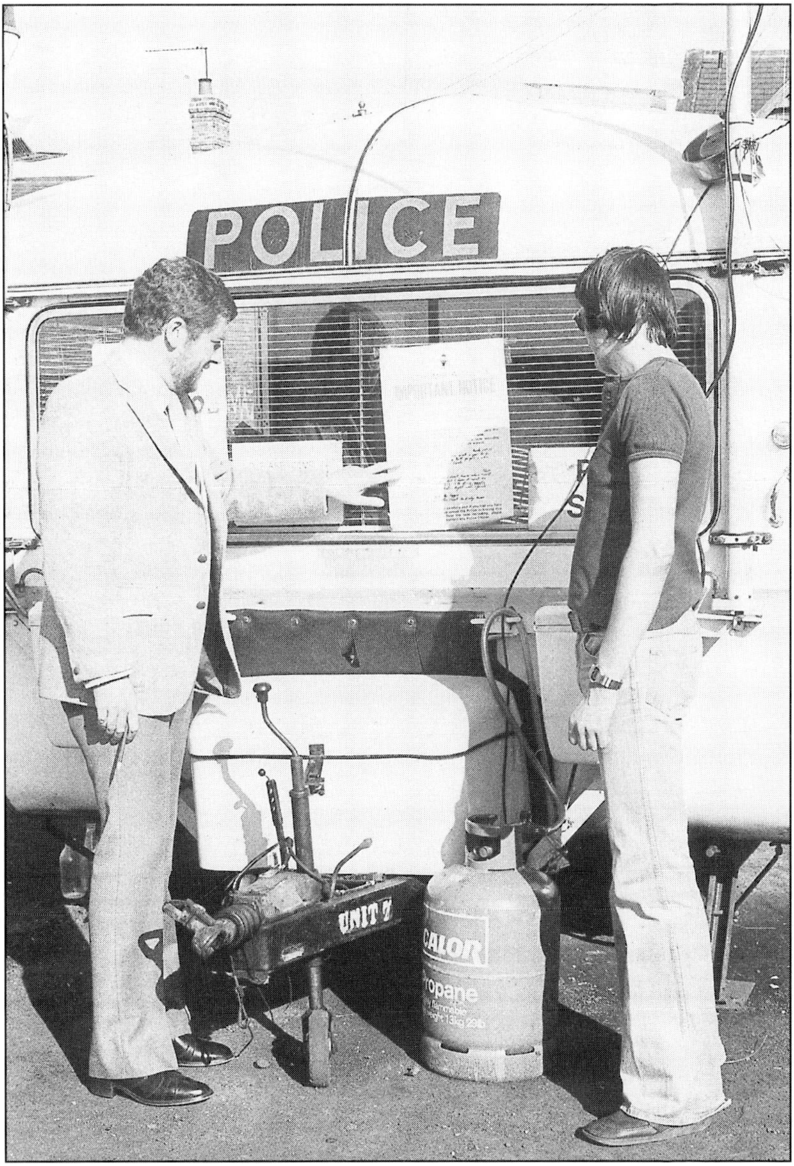

Two Sunderland Ripper Squad detectives read a poster offering a reward for information in the hunt for Wearside Jack/the Yorkshire Ripper on the window of the police caravan that toured the north of Sunderland. Picture: *The Sunderland Echo*.

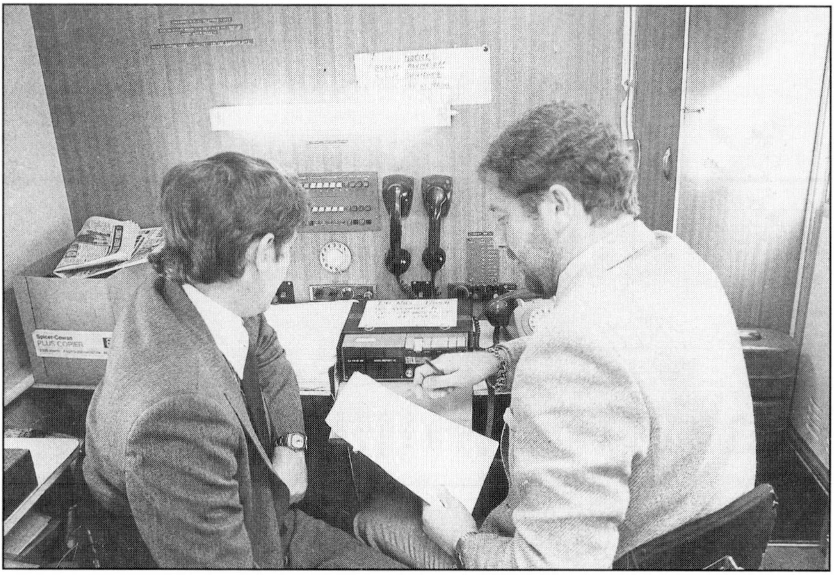

Two detectives listen to the hoax "I'm Jack" tape inside the police caravan. Picture: *The Sunderland Echo.*

Det Con Virtue, who still lives in Sunderland, says: "In the 29 years I have been in the police force I have never seen as much publicity as there was for this inquiry. It was incredible. We hadn't been working long when another murder came in. Somebody rang me and told me I could expect a big media interest in the case again.

"It was always in the back of everybody's mind that the tape could have been a hoax. But, like everything else, our job was riddled with problems. Once we got started, though, we had to get on with it, in a professional way, or we didn't do it at all. The thought about whether or not it was a hoaxer didn't come into it."

The experienced detective adds: "I have worked on a number of murder inquiries - at least six or seven - and the slightest little thing can detect the killer. I was off this particular inquiry before the Ripper was arrested."

Sunderland's Ripper Squad police officers became familiar faces in Castletown, Hylton Castle, and on the surrounding estates. Det Con Virtue recalls that all the local people were willing to help them as much as they could. He says: "Everyone in Castletown helped us. They were great.

"There were media people, from all over the country, coming to Castletown. The local people did not get upset about the police inquiry, but they were a bit narked about the Press coverage."

Not all the media coverage of the hunt for the Ripper/Wearside Jack was negative. Det Con Virtue recalls the regional and local Press did everything they could to help. Sunderland Echo photographer Kevin Brady says he and a reporter would visit the Town End Farm base of the Ripper Squad "almost every day" to find out if there were any developments in the case.

Retired Detective Constable Gordon Clark, who spent 18 months on the inquiry, says the regional journalists, particularly those who worked in regional television, went out of their way to help police. And he recalls one particular day when popular television news anchorman Mike Neville personally helped police to search through film library footage at the BBC's base in Newcastle.

North East television news presenter Mike Neville, who was with the BBC at the time of the Ripper inquiry and is now the anchorman for Tyne Tees Television's main evening regional news. Picture: *The Sunderland Echo*.

Mr Clark says: "It was when we were touring the hospitals trying to find a man and eliminate him from the inquiry. Someone remembered the man might have featured in a snippet on the regional news.

"We went down to Tyne Tees Television and the BBC in Newcastle to ask if we could look through tapes of their old bulletins, and everyone went out of their way to help us. I met Mike Neville. He's a real gentleman. He assisted us personally. There were quite a few tapes to look through.

"We got to know the people working in television quite well. So well, in fact, we were invited to parties they held."

There were other, lighter, moments during the long inquiry which came as a welcome, albeit temporary, diversion for police officers, when local people who generally like to "tell it as it is" made certain comments to officers. These were repeated to others back at the Ripper Squad base or in the parade or briefing room at Gill Bridge Police Station. Despite the intensity of the inquiry, police were also able to retain their sense of humour.

Mr Clark recalls sitting in the briefing room at Gill Bridge when he and other Ripper Squad officers were shown slides on an overhead projector of certain items - he can't say what - found at the scene of some of the murders. Each of the items was shown on a slide next to a ruler, to give police some indication of the measurement of the item.

He says: "The briefings were sometimes lighthearted. On this one occasion when the slides were shown one of the officers said 'This fella will be caught easily ... he drops rulers everywhere he goes'. He didn't say it that loudly but it did cause a ripple of laughter in the briefing room."

On the streets of Castletown and Hylton Castle officers on house-to-house inquiries often picked up a funny tale to relate to their colleagues.

Mr Clark also worked knocking on doors and talking to local people. One day he and a colleague were knocking on every door in a very long street in Hylton Castle asking people if they thought they might know who Wearside Jack/the Yorkshire Ripper was. Or if they had any suspicions about any local characters.

He says: "During that stage of the inquiry I was working with a detective from Newcastle. He was about 6ft tall, with blond hair and wore gold-rimmed spectacles. We were both wearing suits, shirts and ties, and, of course, we were carrying our clipboards.

"On every other door we knocked the residents would tell us their suspicions about two local men, who were living in the street. They were obese, a little scruffy, a little reclusive. Basically they weren't the full shilling. At the end of the day they proved to be harmless.

"When we arrived at their front door, which had a glass panel in it, we knocked and we could see two figures in the passageway. We heard one of them say, 'It's them again, the Mormons or the bloody Jehova's Witnesses'.

"They probably thought that because of our suits and clipboards. Anyway, they opened the door and we told them we weren't Jehova's Witnesses or Mormons and that we were police officers. They let us in and we interviewed them.

"They were moaning about being pestered by religious people knocking at the door and when we left, just for a joke, I said, ' Have they not converted you yet?'. One of the men looked straight at me, all serious like, and said, 'What are you talking about? We've had natural gas for years!"

One detective, who wishes to remain anonymous, says: "I remember being told about a certain detective sergeant who went out to a house with a colleague to interview a local man. When a woman answered the door she immediately said, 'You're tecs aren't you' and the officer asked how she knew that. She replied that there was only two kinds of men who wore a suit, shirt and tie. One was a detective, she said, and the other was Mark Phillips!"

Another officer, again anonymous, says: "For most people in Castletown it was the first time they had had a police officer coming to talk to them on their doorsteps. Often, when we called, they would just ask, 'Are you from the Ripper inquiry'? They knew what we were after and we never came across any hostility. The people of Castletown were really great. They were a little suspicious at first but it became a real talking point for everyone in the village when they went to the clubs at the weekends."

Gordon Lilley, 74, a former councillor who has lived in Castletown all his life, says the hunt for the Ripper/Wearside Jack was THE topic of conversation in Castletown Workingmen's Club and what is known locally as "The Mickey Mouse". The "Mickey Mouse", he says, is the small bar in what is now the Billy Hardy Sports Centre in Castletown. Mr Lilley says: "It was nicknamed the Mickey Mouse because that's what it is ... Mickey Mouse. It's only a very small bar and if you get 30 people in, it's packed.

"The Ripper inquiry and the interest being shown by police and the media was the talk of the village. The whole village was buzzing," says Mr Lilley.

But Sunderland's Ripper Squad never lost sight of the fact that Wearside Jack may have moved out of the area. And in 1979 and 1980 the net was widened to other areas of the North East. Hundreds of men in outlying towns and villages were questioned.

And, in one of the most bizarre twists to the Ripper inquiry, scores of people throughout the North East who were never interviewed had their facial characteristics examined by detectives without their knowledge. That strange twist to the story of Wearside Jack - never before made public - can now be revealed for the first time.

CHAPTER SIX

Pits, Pubs, Clubs and ...Beer Mats

Detective Constable George Virtue played the Wearside Jack tape at pits across the North East and in pubs and workingmen's clubs. In the collieries, he would often play the tape at the pithead baths where miners, some wearing nothing but a coat of coal dust, would listen to the dulcet tones of Jack as they showered following their shift.

He says: "I covered virtually all the pits; Wearmouth, in Sunderland, Vane Tempest, at Seaham, Herrington, Easington. I can't remember any in the area where I didn't play the tape. A lot of the time I would have to play the tape in the changing rooms at the pithead baths where the men were showering.

"The main incident room was at Gill Bridge and I was always backwards and forwards. I was using my own car at the time. There were some days I was still at the pits up until 1am.

"Generally, all the miners co-operated and they would sit and listen to the tape. I had my own tape recorder. Some would sit on the benches and some would listen to it while they were taking a shower."

There were scores of collieries in the North East, particularly in the old Durham coalfield area. But the playing of the tape yielded few clues as to the identity of Jack. Sunderland Ripper Squad police also had no luck playing the tape in pubs and clubs.

Det Con Virtue says: "Part of my job was going around the clubs playing the tape and going to other areas, outside of Sunderland, after they decided everyone born in certain districts of Sunderland had to be interviewed and eliminated from the inquiry.

"I remember a lot of people had moved from Sunderland to Peterlee and other new towns, such as Washington, so I would find myself travelling to and from those areas to interview people.

"I took the tape around virtually all the workingmen's clubs in the area. Pallion, the Catholic Club in Tatham Street, Red House, Castletown, Southwick. I did them all. One that sticks in my mind is the Southwick club. I remember I was asked to go there on a Sunday night because BBC Television was going to be there. I think they were going out live at the time.

"The club committee men, out of courtesy, would put a table out for us, and after we played the tape we would ask people to come and talk to us if they recognised the voice. I can't remember many that did. There wasn't a lot of people that came forward. We used to play the tape between about 7pm and 8pm."

One of the semi-professional singers touring the pubs and workingmen's clubs in the North East at the time was John Gaffney, who says, with a degree of pride, that best selling novelist Dame Catherine Cookson - Our Kate, as she was affectionately known in the North East - said he was the best singer she had ever heard.

Mr Gaffney, of Sunderland, is a former Merchant Navy seaman but had to leave the job in 1992 and take early retirement after an accident in a ship's engine room when he slipped and fell. Dame Catherine once told BBC Radio Newcastle's Golden Hour presenter Frank Wappat that Mr Gaffney had the "most beautiful voice I have ever heard". Our Kate made the comment after hearing Mr Gaffney, a talented baritone, singing the song "*Journey's End*", which was originally a B side by Al Martino.

Dame Catherine Cookson, "Our Kate", who once said John Gaffney had the most beautiful voice she had ever heard. Picture: *The Sunderland Echo.*

In the 1970s and 1980s Mr Gaffney, who used the stage name Johnny Dawn, also entered many talent contests, singing country and western, rock and roll and ballads. One highlight of his career was when he appeared at the London Palladium when he won a national talent contest organised by a popular Sunday newspaper. He won all categories in the contest and walked away with a £1,000 top prize and offers of work came flooding in.

It was through his singing that he met his wife, Mary. The couple met when Mr Gaffney was resident singer at The Alexandra pub in Grangetown, Sunderland. During the 1970s and 1980s, touring the pubs and clubs during breaks in his Merchant Navy career, Johnny Dawn became one of the North East's top acts.

Talented local singer and artist John Gaffney, who used the stage name Johnny Dawn. Ripper Squad officers were interested in looking at scores of sketches by Mr Gaffney, which he drew on beer mats in local pubs and clubs. Picture: *John Gaffney*.

But Mr Gaffney had another artistic skill which gives us one of the most fascinating, and bizarre, stories to emerge during the Sunderland Ripper Squad's hunt for Wearside Jack/the Yorkshire Ripper. It is a story Mr Gaffney has shared only with his wife during the last 20 years.

Mr Gaffney is a talented artist and when he was touring the pubs and clubs of the North East in the 1970s and early 1980s he would spend his time, when not on stage, making sketches of ordinary people who were sitting in the audience or standing at the bar. Mr Gaffney admits that some of his subjects did not realise they were being sketched.

His collection of beer mat sketches, intricate in detail, became known to the police and they believed they might just provide that longed-for lead in the hunt for Wearside Jack/the Yorkshire Ripper. Perhaps Mr Gaffney had actually drawn the face of the Ripper on one of the beer mats?

Mr Gaffney says: "I have always liked drawing and sketching. I sometimes use ink with water and I have tried my hand at painting watercolours. But when I was touring the pubs and workingmen's clubs in the North East I used to just sketch people on a beer mat, using a biro or a pencil. Most knew I was sketching them but some didn't realise.

"I remember once I was in a club in Durham and I started sketching a man sitting there with a woman. He came up to me and asked what I was doing. I told him I was sketching and he looked at the beer mat and said, 'That's me'. Then he said, 'Are you going to tell her husband?' But that was the only time there was ever any trouble about what I was doing.

"I played the Farringdon Club in Sunderland, Pennywell, Red House, Castletown, the Ivy Leaf Club in Hendon and all the local clubs in Durham. I don't think there was one club in the whole of Sunderland and County Durham where I didn't play. And in all of them I would sketch people during my breaks off stage."

Mr Gaffney says: "Somebody had told the police about it and they arrived at my house and said they wanted to look at the beer mats. They took them all away but returned most of them after a few days. There were five or six of them which they kept hold of for a few days longer. I think one or two of them I did in the Park Lane lounge in Sunderland. The police had put them to one side and kept them in a small brown envelope.

"They must have had a description of the person they were looking for and thought they might be able to trace him from the sketches. I remember a lot of lorry drivers used to park up at Park Lane and go for a pint in the Park Inn or the Park Lane lounge. That's probably why the police were so interested in the five or six they held on to.

"At the time they didn't tell me who they were looking for. But later my wife said they probably thought I had sketched the Ripper. At the time, people in Sunderland were very wary of strangers. Anyone unfamiliar who walked into the pubs and clubs were looked at with suspicion.

"Some people did get annoyed when they found out I was sketching them. It almost came to fisticuffs once or twice. But when they had a look at the sketch they seemed to be quite impressed and I let some people have them."

All the beer mats were eventually returned to Mr Gaffney. It is not known why the police were so interested in six of the sketches, but there is a resemblance in all the subjects to the Yorkshire Ripper, Peter Sutcliffe.

The six beer mat sketches detectives retained for several days:

Mr Gaffney sketched this man in the Park Lane Lounge in Sunderland town centre. He believes the man was a lorry driver.

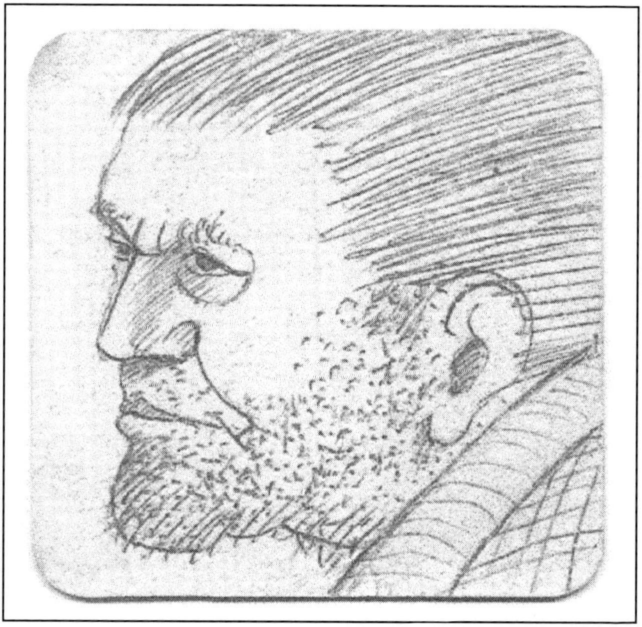

The sketch of this man was done at Seaham Workingmen's Club, one of two drawn at the club which were of particular interest to the Ripper Squad.

This sketch, of an old miner, was done at the Seaham Workingmen's Club in Seaham, County Durham, on the outskirts of Sunderland.

Mr Gaffney drew a sketch of this man in the Park Lane lounge. He recalls the man was a travelling salesman of some sort and delivered goods to Sunderland's Civic Centre.

This man was sketched at the RAOB Club in Silksworth, Sunderland. The club is known locally as "The Buffs".

Mr Gaffney sketched this man at the Theatre Tavern in Lambton Street, Sunderland. He was interested in the man's face because, with him being a country and western singer, he said the man looked like an older Kenny Rogers.

CHAPTER SEVEN

Bodily Fluids and Footprints

If the murder in Preston in November, 1975, of 26-year-old mother-of-two Joan Harrison provided Ripper Squad detectives with clues as to the identity of her killer, the clues did not point fully to Peter William Sutcliffe.

Sutcliffe is of the B blood group and the murderer of Joan Harrison was a B secretor. Sutcliffe admitted killing 13 women and attempting to kill seven more. Did he really have anything to lose by admitting the killing of Joan Harrison? Most observers think not.

The Assistant Chief Constable of West Yorkshire, George Oldfield, who headed the Ripper inquiry, was convinced Wearside Jack was the Yorkshire Ripper for a number of reasons.

He knew, and it could be proved, that the killer of Joan Harrison and the sender of the letters and tape was a B secretor. Of that there is no doubt. Mr Oldfield also believed Mrs Harrison's murder was the work of the Ripper.

Another reason was information about the murders in one of the hoax letters which he said could only be known by the killer.

The extracts from the letters released by police were only extracts. The crucial piece of information which convinced Mr Oldfield, and other senior West Yorkshire officers, that Wearside Jack was the Ripper was never made public.

For the first time, and after 20 years, that information can now be revealed.

According to a senior Ripper Squad detective, in one of the three letters - believed to be the one sent to Mr Oldfield in March, 1979 - the author made known something that had not been reported in the newspapers or in the broadcast media.

What Wearside Jack said, according to the officer, was that he remembered being with Vera Millward, a 41-year-old prostitute, who was murdered by the Ripper in Manchester and found dead in May, 1978.

The critical piece of information Jack told officers was that he recalled sitting with Mrs Millward, when she told him she had had treatment at a certain local hospital.

Detectives in West Yorkshire checked the hospital records and it was revealed the woman had, in fact, had treatment at that hospital, as Wearside Jack had stated. The senior Ripper Squad officer said: "That was it. Mr Oldfield went for it, hook, line and sinker."

The B secretor with a gap in his teeth was a lorry driver, aged 20 to 42, living in or born in Castletown, Sunderland, involved in some kind of engineering, who drove a Ford Corsair, an Austin Cambridge or a Morris Oxford, size seven shoes, dark hair with a beard, known to have links with prostitutes, possibly left handed, sexually perverse, possessing a copy of the song *"Thank you for Being A Friend"*, by Andrew Gold, and a tape recorder and with a distinctive Sunderland accent. From where did detectives draw up this offender profile?

The Sunderland accent and the fact he was a B secretor came from the hoax tape and letters. Linguistics expert Stanley Ellis also suggested he was aged 20 to 42.

From forensic evidence at the scene of Joan Harrison's murder - mistakenly thought to be the work of the Ripper - came corroboration that her killer was a B secretor and that he had links with prostitutes.

More corroboration that he had links with prostitutes was apparent from the information in one of the letters that finally convinced Mr Oldfield that Wearside Jack was the Yorkshire Ripper.

How could he have known that Mrs Millward - a prostitute and one of the Ripper's victims - had attended a certain hospital for treatment? He must have known the woman to be as specific as that.

What about the lorry driver and link with engineering clues? Two of those clues came from the scene of the murder of building society clerk Josephine Anne Whitaker, in early April, 1979. She was murdered in a park in Halifax and, according to the senior Ripper Squad detective, who wishes to remain anonymous, the clues connected the killer to driving and engineering.

The officer says: "At the scene of the murder of the girl from Halifax were lots of footprints left by the Ripper. The ground must have been soft. Some of the topsoil was taken away for forensic analysis and it was found that the killer had been wearing boots with a common commando-style sole.

The Assistant Chief Constable of West Yorkshire, George Oldfield (left) on one of his many visits to Sunderland, talking to the head of Sunderland CID, Detective Superintendent Peter Docherty. Picture: *The Sunderland Echo.*

"All the detectives working on the case were shown these footprints and that's why we would ask to see boots when we called into homes to eliminate people. Forensic also found some type of engineering oil at the scene.

"The sole on the right footprint was found to be more worn down than that of the left and this was the evidence that suggested the killer was a lorry driver. It was the oil that suggested he also had something to do with engineering."

The senior Ripper Squad officer adds: "I remember there was a suggestion from one of the officers at the time that the killer might be someone who goes parachuting quite regularly, because parachutists always land on their right foot first, and that could have been why the right boot was more worn down than the left.

"It was suggested that a team of officers should be sent up to the old Sunderland airport to examine the land there. Some officers thought taking that suggestion seriously was unbelievable. I don't know for sure if that was done. But I wouldn't have been surprised."

What about the suggestion that the murderer was left-handed? An autopsy on one of the victims - a tall woman - made police officers believe the hammer blows were struck in an upward motion by someone left-handed because of the nature of her injuries.

Peter Sutcliffe did kill Josephine Whitaker in the park in Halifax and he did kill Vera Millward, whom Wearside Jack said had told him she had had treatment at a certain hospital. He has always denied killing Joan Harrison and was eliminated from the inquiry because of the forensic evidence.

What about the make of car? Tyre marks found at the scene of the murder of Yvonne Pearson, a 22-year-old killed in Bradford in January, 1978, gave police investigators who specialise in vehicle and traffic inquiries the wheel base of the car involved. It was either a Ford Corsair, an Austin Cambridge or a Morris Oxford.

Sutcliffe did drive a Ford Corsair and he did kill Yvonne Pearson.

Where does that leave us in the hunt for Wearside Jack?

The clues at the scene of the Halifax murder can be disregarded. It cannot be said that Wearside Jack was a lorry driver who wore boots with common commando style soles and was somehow linked to engineering. Those clues pointed only to Sutcliffe.

The clues at the scene of the murder of Yvonne Pearson can, again, be disregarded. There was nothing to suggest Jack drove one of the three suspected cars. That clue only pointed to Sutcliffe.

What about the description he had a beard? That came from witness descriptions to police. In March, 1975, a woman who was attacked by Sutcliffe, but survived, gave detectives one of the first descriptions of the serial killer, who had a beard.

It is the clues that remain that point to Wearside Jack: The blood group (he was a B secretor); he was aged 20 to 42; he had a gap in his top two front teeth; he had a lisp; he was from Wearside; he had links with prostitutes, was sexually perverse; probably hated women, and he travelled occasionally from Wearside to West Yorkshire. There was his handwriting to go on and the fact that he possessed a copy of the Andrew Gold record *"Thank You for Being a Friend".*

When Vera Millward pointed to a hospital and told Wearside Jack she had had treatment there it leaves us with three possibilities. Jack knew Vera Millward well enough for her to give him that information; the hospital line had already been in the newspapers (some officers believed it had); or Jack had taken a shot in the dark, and hit the target.

Between June, 1979, and January, 1981, the evidential links which were later found to point to two different men, Jack and Sutcliffe, pointed only to one; the Yorkshire Ripper, who was born, grew up or lived in Sunderland. And it was on Sunderland that hundreds of detectives concentrated their in-depth inquiries.

At the time many police officers were involved in taking samples of saliva from potential suspects and samples of handwriting. The work was laborious, time-consuming and, at the end of the day, pointless, because they never got a result. But some had interesting stories to tell.

Retired Detective Constable Gordon Clark, of the Sunderland Ripper Squad, was one of the officers touring the North East to collect saliva samples.

Mr Clark was a uniformed constable for three years but spent the rest of his 26-year police career with CID in Sunderland. He joined the force in 1966, when it was the Durham Constabulary, and was stationed initially in Bishop Auckland. He moved to Sunderland in 1969 when he married his wife Pat.

Mr Clark says: "What they did was pair us off with a detective from Yorkshire. We had our local knowledge, such as locations and a lot of information on local people, so we would go around with the detective from West Yorkshire and carry out the actions; basically finding people and eliminating them from the inquiry.

"A record was made of all the names and addresses and these people needed to be seen and eliminated from the inquiry. Each action was very time consuming. Sometimes it took between an hour and two hours.

"A lot of the work I had to do was outside of the area. I covered the whole of the North East really. What would happen is that someone would have knocked on a door, say in Red House,

Retired Detective Constable Gordon Clark, of the Sunderland Ripper Squad. Picture: *Patrick Lavelle.*

and found out that the person we were looking for had moved, to Consett, Chester-le-Street, or wherever.

"I would then have to follow that up and go outside of the area to eliminate them. I did about 100 actions outside of Sunderland. I went to places such as North Tyneside and Weardale and Willington in County Durham.

"I also did the mental hospitals. There was one at Newton Aycliffe and I also did Sunderland's psychiatric hospital, Cherry Knowle, in Ryhope. At that time I was working with a Detective Constable Tommy Boyd, who I think was from Whitley Bay.

"One of the actions turned out to be a bit strange. We were told to go to Cherry Knowle to see this bloke. We got on to the ward and we were greeted by the staff nurse and two male nurses. We expected then to be taken to see the patient in his bed.

"We were told the man we wanted to see was in the grounds of the hospital. So we looked out of the window and it looked as if he was trying to make love to the daisies. His backside was going up and down. It was obvious to us that the man had serious mental health problems, we couldn't interview him, so we just left.

"For several months my job was going around collecting saliva samples. I did hundreds of them. What with that, and having to go around the mental hospitals, it shows how I always got the shit end of the stick.

"We took the samples mainly from men who couldn't read or write, because they still had to be eliminated from the inquiry. And, of course, we were looking for a B secretor. The samples would be sent off to the laboratory at Wetherby for forensic examination.

"The sample bottles were about the same size as those used for urine samples. But a few people we asked must have thought they had to fill the thing with saliva, rather than just give us a drop.

"One of the first samples I took was quite horrific. There was a miner living in Thorney Close, Sunderland, and we went out early in the morning to see him. When I arrived at the house he was sitting there sucking on a Woodbine.

"We told him what we wanted; he heaved once or twice and brought up this conflagration from the bottom of his lungs and spit it all out into the container. It was every colour of the rainbow. It was disgusting.

"There was another we took from a chap after he had just eaten his breakfast. I sent it off but it was returned, from Wetherby, with a message from the lab which said, 'Can we have a sample of saliva next time rather than a sample of Weetabix'.

"Another one I remember we took from a man who had just had all his teeth out. It was pure blood. The scientists, and I don't know why, were unable to tell if he was a B secretor from the blood. They needed saliva."

Mr Clark adds: "When we visited people's homes for samples it had to be unannounced. We couldn't just ring them up and tell them we wanted a sample of their saliva to eliminate them from the Ripper inquiry. That's why, on many, we went early morning.

"One day we went to Willington in County Durham to take a sample from a man there. When we turned up he was shocked and suspicious. He started to sweat, he went red, and he dried up. He couldn't give us a sample.

"Sometimes, just for a joke, when we got the samples I would go into Davey Zak's office and slowly roll them on to his desk. He used to jump out of his chair in disgust and sometimes leave the room."

Mr Clark's work proved fruitless. It never did lead to the capture of the Yorkshire Ripper - he was caught by police on routine patrol. And Wearside Jack? He could still be on Wearside, or he could be dead.

CHAPTER EIGHT

Assisting with Inquiries

With many murders over several years to investigate, the hunt for the Yorkshire Ripper was always a West Yorkshire Police inquiry. But after Wearside Jack sent George Oldfield the hoax letters and taunting tape, the whole focus of the investigation switched, almost overnight, from the Ripper's stalking ground around Manchester, Halifax, Bradford and Leeds, to Wearside and, in particular, the area north of the River Wear.

In the local and regional Press, Northumbria Police was reported to be doing all it could to assist colleagues from the North West and detectives and uniformed officers in Sunderland had their work cut out more than most.

According to a Ripper Squad detective, Sunderland police officers were drafted into the massive inquiry "almost overnight".

And George Oldfield's confidence, persistence even, in believing Jack was the Ripper was not mirrored on Wearside, he says, where many senior officers, and frontline bobbies on house-to-house inquiries, still had firmly in their mind's eye the notion that they were on the hunt for a sick hoaxer, not a serial killer.

The Ripper officer, who does not wish to be named, says: "We were literally just shot on to the inquiry.

"I remember I was sitting at my desk when the order came down from above. One of the more senior detectives just walked into the office, pointed his finger, and said 'You! You! and You! Get out on the Ripper'. And that was it."

Detective Inspector Dave Zackrisson - or Davey Zack as he was known to the Sunderland Ripper Squad - never believed Wearside Jack was the Yorkshire Ripper and it was he who put together the most powerful and persuasive case against the tape's authenticity.

And there was one particular Ripper murder, which coincided with Jack sending a letter to Mr Oldfield, that Zack thought would convince the senior officers in West Yorkshire that they had been sent on the biggest wild goose chase in British criminal history.

On January 21, 1978, Yvonne Pearson - one of the Ripper's victims - was murdered in Bradford. Wearside Jack posted his first letter to West Yorkshire Police in early March, 1978; it was postmarked Sunderland and dated March 8. Yvonne Pearson's body was found weeks after she was killed - on March 26 - significantly AFTER Jack posted his first letter.

And yet Jack, the supposed serial killer, who loved to taunt police about their inability to catch him, and who, probably, had the best opportunity so far to claim police ineptitude, failed to mention they had yet to discover the body of his latest victim, Yvonne Pearson. Where was the snide comment: "*Your lads are letting you down, George*", now?

Zack saw this, according to the senior Ripper Squad detective, as the best confirmation yet that the Sunderland man was not the Yorkshire Ripper.

Although Zack was regarded by some rank-and-file officers in Sunderland as something of a "college boy" - what frontline police officers now term a "Bramshill high-flyer" - he was an astute detective with sound judgement.

And Sunderland officers paid more attention to his views than they did on anything that anyone from the West Yorkshire end of the inquiry had to say about the case.

The Ripper Squad officer said: "At the morning briefings when there happened to be no West Yorkshire officers in the room, Zak's words to us were always the same and to the point.

"He couldn't say what he had to say in front of West Yorkshire officers, because that would be seen as undermining what, at the end of the day, were the views of their top people. It was a West Yorkshire inquiry and we were assisting.

"Zak would say 'keep an open mind'. And he would say he was not convinced the man who sent the tape and the letters was responsible for the murders. If he was responsible he said that would be a bonus but he always stressed 'for God's sake, keep an open mind'.

"What had convinced him was the earlier letter when the writer failed to mention the body that had lain undiscovered. This man liked to taunt the police and yet he never mentioned that they still hadn't found the body of one of his victims.

"Zak said that if this man was the Ripper he would have definitely mentioned it. He prepared a report on it and sent it to West Yorkshire. This was what he was trying to get through to them."

The officer adds: "In one of the letters the writer said he 'was going to kill an old hag next'. It was thought Sutcliffe did go out and kill an older prostitute after the sending of that letter. But that must have been a coincidence because, as far as I can remember, that bit of information was never made public."

"George Oldfield did attend a few of our briefings and I remember seeing him at least twice. It was thought he had a drink problem and I remember he went into hospital at one stage of the inquiry, I don't know if that was stress-related. The Sunderland lads had a whip-round and we bought him a bottle of whisky."

The officer's claim that Jack failed to mention "his" latest murder in his first letter would explain why police never made the Wearside connection with the killings public until after they received the third letter and the tape. Early inquiries were, however, carried out into people with Sunderland links, particularly those working or travelling to West Yorkshire.

Eventually, several Sunderland officers spent time in West Yorkshire, assisting police there with the inquiry and a team of 12 detectives, seconded to the squad for varying periods of time, worked in Sunderland and stayed at the Roker Hotel on the seafront.

One of the West Yorks officers who worked in Sunderland for about 12 months was Detective Constable Tommy Jackson.

Mr Jackson, originally from Brandon, County Durham, and now retired, applied to join Durham Constabulary when he decided on a police career in 1968. He wanted to remain living in County Durham where he met his wife, Joyce.

But Durham Constabulary was one of the only forces in the country, at that time, which was not recruiting constables. Mr Jackson had gone through all the preliminary stages to join the police service and was looking for a way in.

One police magazine was full of job advertisements, so he opened the jobs pages, closed his eyes, and took pot luck ... by sticking a pin in the page.

The pin landed on an advert for recruits for the West Riding Constabulary. Mr Jackson joined the West Riding force as a beat constable and stayed with them. It has always been the same force, but with different names, so Mr Jackson served with the West Riding Constabulary, West Yorkshire Constabulary, West Yorkshire Metropolitan Police and, finally, West Yorkshire Police.

Mr Jackson, 53, and his wife have a daughter and two grandchildren. They still live between Bradford and Leeds and, during the Ripper hunt, Mr Jackson travelled regularly to see relatives back in County Durham.

Retired Detective Constable Tommy Jackson at his home near Bradford, West Yorkshire. Mr Jackson worked on three of the Yorkshire Ripper murders and spent 12 months in Sunderland in the hunt for Wearside Jack. Picture: *Patrick Lavelle.*

At his home it is apparent that Mr Jackson is proud of his North East roots. Pride of place on a living room wall is a striking picture of Durham Cathedral lit up at night. And on the stair landing there hangs an illustration of Vane Tempest Colliery at Seaham, County Durham.

It was because of his North East roots, and his work as a detective constable on three of the Ripper murders in West Yorkshire, that Mr Jackson was assigned to work in Sunderland in 1979.

During the inquiry, solid friendships were formed - and have lasted. Mr Jackson and retired Detective Constable Gordon Clark - also originally from County Durham - have kept in touch since their days on the Ripper Squad.

Mr Jackson was heavily involved in the investigations into the Ripper murders of Irene Richardson, aged 28, killed in Leeds in February, 1977; Helen Rytka, an 18-year-old murdered in Huddersfield in January, 1978; and Josephine Whitaker, the 19-year-old student found dead on playing fields in Halifax in April, 1979.

He says: "I was up in Sunderland first in 1978 and for most of 1979 but came back down to West Yorkshire for three to four months. Then I went back to Sunderland. I was a detective constable at the time and one of the reasons they wanted me to work up north was because I am from County Durham.

"They had the tape and the experts had decided that he came from somewhere north of the river, so what we were doing up there was interviewing thousands of men. I think there were about 50,000 men who needed to be eliminated in total.

"The Ripper tape had been played, so we had people ringing in telling us they thought the voice belonged to whoever. All the names were between a certain age group, I think originally the age range was between late teens up to 55.

"We also had to collect saliva samples and ask people their shoe size and where they were on the dates of the murders, take handwriting samples. We would dicate a passage, then talk for a while, and dictate some more. I think we were taking three handwriting samples, but there may have been only two.

"There were 12 of us up in Sunderland at the time. Sometimes I went around the clubs but later I went around all the pits playing the tape. There were teams of us doing that and I must have covered most of the collieries in the area.

"Obviously it was a monumental task but, at the time, it appeared straightforward. We knew it was going to be a long inquiry."

A Wearside man reads one of the hundreds of posters printed and distributed by the Sunderland Echo to assist police in the hunt for the Yorkshire Ripper/Wearside Jack. Picture: *The Sunderland Echo.*

Mr Jackson adds: "Many of the men we were looking for had been involved in shipbuilding or the coal industry, and some had moved from the North East to the coalfields in Nottingham and Selby. If we found a man had moved there, we would pass the information on to detectives in West Yorkshire.

"I played the tape to thousands of miners in the North East. The first few times we played the tape we would wait at the pithead for the men finishing their shift. When the cage came up it was just like a stampede, and they were heading towards us.

"I would be standing there holding the tape recorder and asking them to listen and see if they recognised the voice. But they were off like a shot and, after the dust had settled, I would be standing there open-mouthed in mid-sentence.

"We then decided we had to go before the shift had started and played the tape in the canteen. This time the miners were very attentive. They would listen to the tape, then one of them would shout, 'Hey, I think I know that voice. Can you play it again?'

"We would play it again and then another miner would say he thought he knew the voice, could we play it a third time? We did, and it became obvious the men were just playing for time because they were ten or 15 minutes into their shift. The pit deputy cottoned on to this and soon had them back to work."

Mr Jackson, who had heard the tape so many hundreds of times he could recite it word-for-word, recalls it was also played in the pubs and clubs around West Yorkshire. He can't forget one night in his local club - it led to a barmaid telling police HE was the Ripper.

He says: "I remember during this time I went back to West Yorkshire for a well-earned rest and I had made arrangements to take my parents out to a local workingmen's club. It was called the Hanging Heaton Workingmen's Club and it was on the outskirts of Dewsbury.

"It was the first time I'd been in the club for quite some time. We got in, got a drink and settled down and then, during the interval, when I went to the bar, some police officers started setting up gear on tables on stage. They were going to play the bloody tape!

"I'd played the thing at the pits and in the clubs so many times, sometimes between 20 and 30 times a day, I couldn't stand it, so I said I had heard the tape so many times I knew if off by heart, and I left the club.

"A barmaid had heard me say that and thought, because of that, and my accent, that I must be the Ripper. She also knew I was a police officer. She contacted police at Dewsbury and they started an investigation. But they didn't trace me for at least three months.

"I remember the day I got the call. The officer in Dewsbury told me the story about the police officer in the club, with the accent, who knew the tape word for word and he asked 'was that you?' When I said it was, he said, 'Thank God for that!"

Detective Constable Gordon Clark was one of the Sunderland officers who spent a few months of the Ripper inquiry working in West Yorkshire.

He says: "I was asked to go down to Bradford, and I did. I was staying in a hotel in the city centre and working out of the local police station. It was Easter time when I went down, but there were other officers from Sunderland working on the case down there. I remember there was a Detective Constable Jimmy Watson, who had been there for some time.

"The idea was if there was anyone from the North East arrested they thought it would be worthwhile having a Sunderland officer there so they knew what they were talking about, not in terms of dialect, but local knowledge.

"One of the first things I was asked to do was go to the police station in Dewsbury where I was told a man from our area had been locked up for being drunk and disorderly. I was to interview him and eliminate him from the Ripper inquiry.

"When I saw him it turned out the fella was from Oban, in Scotland. I don't know what made them think he was from our neck of the woods."

Mr Clark adds: "One thing I noticed in Bradford was that there was very little information coming in from members of the public. That was a complete contrast to what was happening in Sunderland.

"The West Yorkshire officers also appeared to have fewer actions per week. They also seemed to firmly believe the man they were looking for had a Wearside accent. Anyone who didn't have a Sunderland accent, they didn't bother with. To me it appeared the inquiry in West Yorkshire was never as intense as it was in the North East."

Another Ripper Squad officer, who does not wish to be named, recalls having to interview pub and club entertainers in the North East. There was one comedian he remembers well, not because his gags were funny, but because he interviewed him as a Wearside Jack suspect - and the comedian stole some of his jokes.

He says: "I had to get a sample of his handwriting, and one of the lines I had to ask him to write was, 'How's your Elsie getting on in hospital?'. That's because the writer of the hoax letters formed the letters in that sentence in a certain way.

"I had quite a chat with this comedian and told him a couple of jokes. We got on great.

"Two to three weeks later I had to go to a club in South Shields to interview someone else, on an unrelated matter, and who should be on stage but this comedian. He was telling my jokes, and I thought what a bloody cheek!

"Then he started saying to the crowd. 'Hey, guess who's been interviewed by the Ripper squad?..... Me! Me! Can you believe it? They thought I was the Yorkshire Ripper'. Just then I shouted, loudly, 'How's your Elsie!' and he was absolutely gobsmacked. He shouted '****ing hell! They're following me around now!' I spoke to him later off stage and he said he'd nearly shit himself."

Those funny moments were a welcome distraction for the Sunderland Ripper Squad and their colleagues from West Yorkshire. They may have shared the same down-to-earth sense of humour but the views of their respective senior officers in the hunt for the Ripper/Wearside Jack were almost diametrically opposed.

PART TWO

"The Suspects"

CHAPTER NINE

Old Fatso

Grandmother Olive Curry, now in her 70s, is the first to admit she has a one-track mind. For almost 20 years she has been on the trail of Wearside Jack who, she insists, was the Yorkshire Ripper's accomplice in at least one and, probably several, of the murders.

Mrs Curry, a retired canteen worker, claims to have seen both Sutcliffe and Jack - whom she calls "Old Fatso" or "Old FO" for short - at the Fishermen's Mission canteen where she worked in 1978. Sutcliffe did not have a beard at the time, says Mrs Curry.

When Sutcliffe was arrested in January, 1981, and his picture appeared on the national television news, Mrs Curry says she recognised him immediately and, having heard the infamous hoax tape, she immediately linked Sutcliffe to the man with the strong Wearside accent.

So determined was Mrs Curry to prove her claims that she began corresponding with the serial killer in 1984. What started as a "penfriend" relationship soon developed into a friendship and Mrs Curry and her husband, Arthur, regularly visited Sutcliffe at Broadmoor Hospital in Berkshire.

By 1993, Mrs Curry had amassed one of the biggest - if not the biggest - collections of letters penned by Sutcliffe anywhere in the country. She keeps them in a battered old suitcase at her small upstairs flat in North Shields.

I first came across Mrs Curry when, as the Crime Correspondent for The Northern Echo, I was assigned to work on her story. Detectives in West Yorkshire were taking her claims very seriously and three plain clothes officers travelled to North Tyneside to meet Mrs Curry in person and hear her story about Sutcliffe and "Old Fatso".

As the new inquiry progressed, I was able to persuade Mrs Curry to allow me to read about 300 of the letters penned by the Ripper. Their contents were wide-ranging, but generally boring, and Sutcliffe repeatedly claimed never to have met Mrs Curry at the canteen in North Shields or to have had an accomplice.

The letters - which I read and transcribed in my own time - did give an insight into the mind of Sutcliffe and his life in Broadmoor. He was envious of Ronnie Kray, who, he said, didn't have his friends "vetted" and he claimed to have turned down an offer of $500,000 to make a film about his reign of terror.

The Ripper letters also contained a claim that he requested Sir Jimmy Savile to "fix-it" for under-privileged children and they also revealed details of the women who dominated his life. Sutcliffe, arguably the most notorious criminal of the 20th Century had his own thoughts on the crime of the century - he said it was the poll tax.

The letters did contain enough material for a series of features for The Northern Echo but the interesting snippets were buried away in what turned out to be nothing more than a 12-year rant from a raving lunatic. Each letter was either a moan about his treatment in Broadmoor - and to me he appeared to have a cushy life inside - or a boring, self-pitying diatribe about all that is wrong, in his jaundiced view, with the world. After hours of reading his turgid scribblings, I would usually have a cup of tea and a couple of Anadins.

The letters from Sutcliffe to Mrs Curry did give me something to write about. But Mrs Curry never got the answers she wanted from Sutcliffe. He said she was on a "crusade". On one visit to Broadmoor she asked him directly if he had murdered the prostitute Joan Harrison in Preston in 1975. "I did not kill that girl," was his reply. "The police proved they were not my teeth marks."

Mrs Curry hoped that her claims would be proven by detectives from West Yorkshire. But, despite another lengthy inquiry into the hoax tape and letters, they were able to prove only that Sutcliffe could not have been in North Shields on the days that Mrs Curry said he was. Detectives could find nothing to link Sutcliffe with "Old Fatso".

At the time of the renewed inquiry to find Wearside Jack, I travelled to Leeds to meet Detective Superintendent Peter Hudson, who was heading the case. He told me: "Mrs Curry is absolutely genuine in her belief about the man she saw with Peter Sutcliffe. This force takes very seriously the story told to us by Mrs Curry. There is no police officer more than me who would like to apprehend the person responsible."

In my research for this book, I visited Mrs Curry again. Despite the view of senior detectives in West Yorkshire that her story could not be true, Mrs Curry remains adamant that she saw Sutcliffe with Wearside Jack in the summer of 1978. She says she will maintain her story until the bitter end.

She says: "All I want is FO. Three girls died because of him. He was downright evil to do such a thing. How did they never find him? The voice on the tape was him. He had the same lisp in his voice that he had when I spoke to him at the Fishermen's Mission canteen where I worked in 1978. And I still say - in fact, I know - that he used to go there with Peter."

Olive Curry reads one of the 400 or so letters she has received from Peter Sutcliffe over the years at her home in North Shields. Picture: *Patrick Lavelle*.

She adds: "Peter never had a beard at the time. The pair used to pull up in a red flatbed lorry. The lorry had the words 'Little Willy' written on the side. I remember Peter once said to me, 'Can you not find a better job than this' and the man with him did speak from time to time. He had a lisp and was broad Sunderland. He looked like Geoffrey Hughes, who played Eddie Yates the binman in *Coronation Street.*

"Peter was the striking one. He was so clean; a nice looking man and very polite. The man with him was about 5ft 4ins, plump, he looked scruffy, and he had a fawn mac buttoned up to the neck. They came to the canteen so often I would keep them a piece or pie or a scone because they were expected."

Mrs Curry says: "Old FO is a wicked man and I am not going to give up. My family are not happy that I am associated with all this, and with Peter. Peter himself has told me to forget about it, to shut up about it. He has said I seem to be on some kind of crusade to find him. But I will never shut up and the day this man is caught I will shout it from the rooftops.

"He was never up north. He worked with Peter and I am sure he is the man who killed the girl in Preston, Joan Harrison. I have asked Peter about that girl myself and he told me, 'I never killed that girl. I never killed Joan Harrison'. He also told me he never bit the girl and that police had proved it wasn't his teeth marks. He does have a gap in his teeth, but he is not a B secretor.

"I still believe Old FO killed that girl. Why I say it is this. Two men, known to each other, one from Bradford, one from Sunderland, they set off this night and they meet a girl called Joan Harrison. One has sex with the girl and one kills her. One went back to Bradford and one went back to wherever he was staying. Agatha Christie could not have written a plot like that.

Olive Curry had such a detailed description of the man she claimed to be a friend and accomplice of the Yorkshire Ripper, Peter Sutcliffe, Paul Wick was able to sketch this impression of the man Mrs Curry called "Old Fatso". "Old Fatso" is Mrs Curry's name for the man who sent the hoax tape and letters to West Yorkshire Police - otherwise known as Wearside Jack. Detectives re-opened the hoax tape inquiry as a result of her claims but said Sutcliffe's work records showed he could not have been in North Shields on the dates Mrs Curry said she spotted him with "Old Fatso". Illustration: *The Northern Echo.*

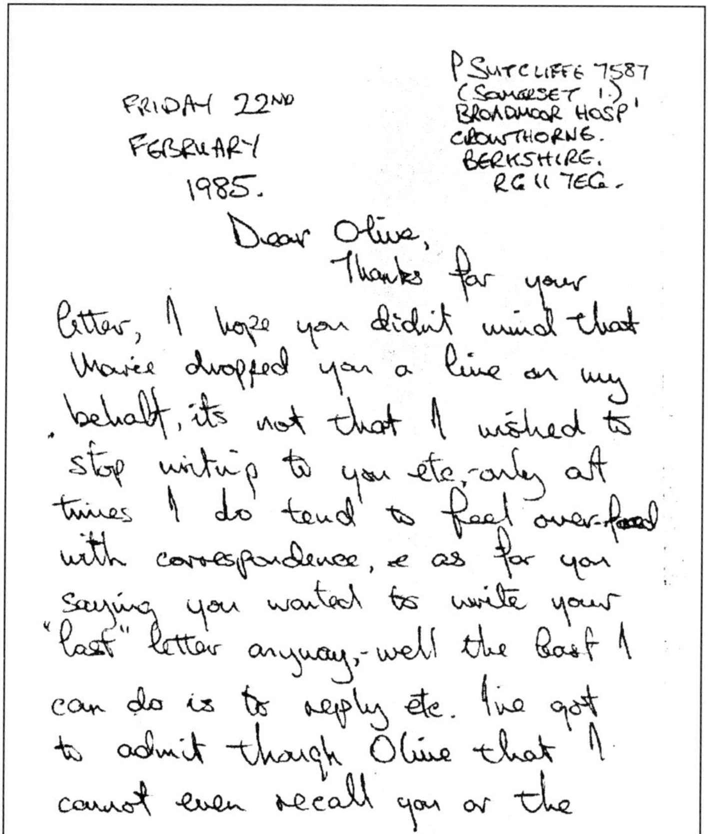

P SUTCLIFFE 7587
(SOMERSET 1.)
BROADMOOR HOSP'
CROWTHORNE.
BERKSHIRE.
RG11 7EG.

FRIDAY 22ND
FEBRUARY
1985.

Dear Olive,

Thanks for your letter, I hope you didn't mind that Maurice dropped you a line on my behalf, its not that I wished to stop writing to you etc, only at times I do tend to feel over-faced with correspondence, & as for you saying you wanted to write your "last" letter anyway, - well the least I can do is to reply etc. I've got to admit though Olive that I cannot even recall you or the

"I've got to admit Olive that I can't even recall you," says Peter Sutcliffe in this letter to Olive Curry dated February, 1985. Mrs Curry has amassed about 400 letters from the Ripper over a period of 15 years. They started off as penpals but Mrs Curry became one of Sutcliffe's closest confidantes.

"Peter never had sex with the girls but the other one did. I've heard there were another two murders that Peter could not have done by himself. I have read as much as I can about it and I can't remember anything about any of the other girls having been bitten. To me, the man who sent the letters and the tape killed Joan Harrison."

Mrs Curry says: "When Peter was arrested in January, 1981, and I saw his face on the television, I recognised him straight away. Then I remembered Old FO being with him at the Fishermen's Mission and I told Arthur, my husband, that I should contact the police. I didn't contact them immediately. I waited some time. But then when I did contact them, they weren't interested.

"They only became interested after I told my story to the Press. Three detectives from West Yorkshire came up to interview me and I told them everything. A few weeks later one of them rang me to say they had looked into it and found that Peter could not have been in North Shields on the dates I had given them. They told me they would come up to explain but I said, 'Don't bother', and I put the 'phone down."

Mrs Curry adds: "The last correspondence I got from Peter was a Christmas card. We stopped writing to each other after I told my story to the Press. But we began writing to each other again, it wasn't a surprise, and then it just came to a halt in October, 1998. I still have all his letters

"My part in all this means that I will not open the door to anybody these days."

The Ripper's Denials

Mrs Curry, whom the Ripper sometimes called 'Lol', has repeatedly put her claims to Sutcliffe that he was linked to Wearside Jack, but the serial killer has always responded by saying he can't recall ever meeting her or having a friend from Sunderland.

In December, 1984, he wrote:

Thanks for your Christmas card. I received so many this year. You mentioned making me a cup of tea, or words to that affect. I've got to admit I've had cups of tea with lots of people, but it's a bit intriguing you have so much to tell me....

Regards Peter.

In February, 1985, he wrote:

I've got to admit, though Olive, that I cannot even recall you, or the Seamen's Mission place you so often refer to... I'm sure you are confusing me with someone else because I know I have never made a 'phone call to any friend in North Shields. I don't know anyone well enough for that, you see. I hope I've helped you get things straightened out etc.

June, 1985.

I can't think what you wish to tell me, as we've quite obviously not met before... I know perfectly well I haven't met you yet and that you're obviously thinking of someone else.

January, 1986.

There's no way I ever knew or even met such a sicko up there, pet. No way at all.

January, 1987.

Oh, Olive, there you go again lass. I've told you your obviously getting mixed up with somebody else. So tis no use gerrin mad at yer pally. There's no way he's going to remember summat that didn't happen.

May, 1987.

Yeah, I do remember you telling me about Old Fatso... You actually mean it's someone you really know?

October, 1988.

About the guy you keep telling me about, Fatso. Well, I would never keep anything from you, there's no way I would do that. So you'll have to take my word for it, that's all. All you have said to me about Fatso is meaningless to me... I've an absolute excellent memory Lol and there's absoutely nowt blocked out.

In December, 1992, the crime reporter at the Sunderland Echo, Nigel Green, wrote to Sutcliffe asking him about Mrs Curry's claims. Sutcliffe wrote back to say Mrs Curry was "obsessed" with the idea. "It's not true!" stated Sutcliffe. The headline on the front page of the Sunderland Echo that day was: "Ripper Denies Wear Mate".

Peter Sutcliffe regarded Olive Curry as such a good friend, he painted this picture, from a photograph, of Mrs Curry and her late husband, Arthur. Sutcliffe stopped writing to Mrs Curry in 1993 after she had spoken to the Press about her claims that he was linked to Wearside Jack, the man who sent police the hoax letters and tape. Picture: *The Northern Echo*.

CHAPTER TEN

Are You Jack?

In the hunt for the Yorkshire Ripper any man with a Wearside accent, aged between 20 and 42, and with links, however tenuous, with Yorkshire could become a potential suspect in the long-running inquiry.

The friends and relatives of those interviewed living locally might have raised doubts about the "suspect" but detectives working on the case pointed the finger more firmly at Sunderland men living and working away from their home town. Even if they had been eliminated from the inquiry without being interviewed, the ex-patriate Mackems found themselves the butt of jokes in the workplace or the subject of animated bar room banter.

"Hey, it's Jack the Ripper!", was often heard in the pubs around Manchester, Leeds, Preston and Bradford, if a Sunderland man was heard ordering a pint at the bar. The Sunderland, or Mackem, dialect - mainly because of Wearside Jack - was instantly recognisable. At least one Sunderland man was refused a pint in a pub in Manchester because the barmaid was convinced he was the Yorkshire Ripper.

Hundreds of Wearside men were interviewed as potential suspects, or at least to be eliminated from the inquiry. Some were able to easily provide an alibi - such as the detective, interviewed three times, who happened to be working on another murder inquiry when Sutcliffe struck. But others had great difficulty persuading detectives they had nothing to do with the murders.

There was the human cost, too.

Many of the "suspects" were anxious to clear their names and concerned that they were being interviewed in the first place. For those interviewed more than once, the experience proved stressful. Their wives or partners may have never seriously doubted their innocence but, some of the wives say now, there was always that "little seed of doubt". The Wearside Jack inquiry planted the foundations for the break-up of at least one marriage.

Wearside Jack had put Sunderland in the national spotlight for all the wrong reasons. Hundreds of innocent men were put in the frame as potential suspects for arguably, at least in Britain, the crime of the century.

Hundreds of men had to have their voices taped for analysis, their handwriting analysed, or had to bite into a mould so forensic scientists could compare the bite marks to those found on the left breast of a dead prostitute. Hundreds had to give police samples of their own bodily fluids by spitting into a specimen bottle. Some found that particular task a little undignified, to say the least, and rather embarrassing.

For the first time, and after 20 years, many of the "suspects" - and I use the term loosely - have dusted the cobwebs from their memories and have spoken about the impact the Wearside Jack inquiry had on their lives.

These are their stories...

Jack the Coalman

Divorced father-of-three Ron Fulbirg, originally from Elswick, Newcastle, but now living in Sunderland, lived and worked in Bradford at the time of the Ripper murders. He was a self-employed coalman, delivering coal in and around the city and the wife of one of his customers suggested police interview him because he has a distinctive gap in his top front teeth.

He says:

'I lived in Bradford at the time and I was running my own coal business, delivering coal around the Laisterdyke estate and the Denholme area. I was self-employed and I had my own wagon. I actually worked out of the British Fuel Company site.

I was born in Elswick, Newcastle, and in the mid 1970s I went down to Bradford to live with my brother, Robert, who had a flat and owned the coal delivery business. We used to go for a drink in the local pubs and also went out dancing and that.

My brother decided to pack the business in and put it up for sale, so we did a deal. I leased the business from him and put so much back into it until I had raised enough cash to buy it. Eventually I took the business over.

One of the deliveries I made on the round was at a farm in the Denholme area. The farmer's wife rang the police to say I looked like the Ripper because of the gap in my teeth. At first I was interviewed voluntarily but, later, I was arrested and questioned on suspicion of murder.

I remember one of the murders they questioned me about was that of a student around the Halifax area. I was stunned. The first thing that I said to police was that I wanted to make a telephone call and I wanted my solicitor present.

They had taken me down for questioning at the main police station in Bradford city centre. At the time my brother and my solicitor were with me and the police kept me in overnight.

The following day I was taken back to my house by two detectives and they actually searched my house. They took a pair of boots, a hammer and some old clothes which were covered in coal dust. I had been burning the clothes in a 45-gallon oil drum which I used for burning rubbish. The detectives said they were taking all the gear away for forensic testing.

It was no good trying to wash the clothes that I used for work. They were so dirty I would just burn them.

Because I have this gap in my teeth and I had a Geordie accent and travelled from the North East to West Yorkshire and because I was a lorry driver, in their eyes I was the most likely suspect at the time.

I was interviewed by police 14 times. I was interviewed by detectives from Harrogate, York, Halifax, Huddersfield, Bradford and by detectives from the North East. From the start I had put two and two together and realised I was being questioned about the Ripper murders.

The strange thing is I had actually met Maureen Long - she was one of the women who, I think, got away from the Ripper - when I was working as a bouncer in a nightclub in the Manningham Lane area of Bradford. It was prostitutes' paradise then and it still is. As I was working in the clubs until the early hours I got to know the girls.

Maureen Long was well-known in the Manningham Lane area and at the time of the killings she was calling for better protection for prostitutes.

When Sutcliffe was done, nobody came back to me and said, 'Right, you are eliminated from the inquiry'. To me that means I am still a suspect in the inquiry for the man who sent the tape. When I was interviewed, as well as listening to my accent, they asked me to write something down because he had also sent them letters.

Some of the detectives were all right, some of them weren't. They had got it into their mind that I looked like the guy and 'let's get this case finished'. Had they never caught Sutcliffe I would still be protesting my innocence. If they hadn't caught Sutcliffe, I could have been up for it.

They got me to record my voice onto a tape and they sent the tape away to be looked at by some experts. The voice on the tape did not coincide with mine. In them days I spoke with a strong Geordie accent, which is a completely different accent from Sunderland.

One thing that had always puzzled me was why was I interviewed 14 times and yet my brother, who has a strong North East accent, was never questioned. I also couldn't fathom out why they were so interested about the gap in my teeth.

About five years ago, when I was working for Homeworthy in Sunderland, I was delivering down south and I stopped in a village, parked up, went to a pub and got talking about all this to a prison officer who was in the same prison where Sutcliffe was.

I told him what I had gone through and he gave me Sutcliffe's address, with all the details, so I could write to him and explain what I had gone through because of him. This prison officer told me Sutcliffe would probably write back, but I never bothered in the end. Whoever sent the tape caused a lot of aggravation and a lot of heartache at the time. My problem was that I fitted the description and I had a North East accent. Many men from the North East who were living in West Yorkshire were questioned about it.

It is unbelievable what I went through at the time of the killings. What I want now is for a police officer to come and tell me I have been eliminated from all their inquiries. I also want the stuff back that they took from my house. ’

Jack the Pitman

Former miner Ken McKone, 59, a divorced father-of-two, originally from South Shields and now living in Seaham, County Durham, was interviewed by detectives three times during the inquiry. He was living alone in a flat in Prestwich, near Preston, at the time, and working long shifts in the local pits as a member of the National Coal Board's area salvage team.

He says:

‘ I had spent most of my life living in the North East and after I left the Merchant Navy I spent a couple of years down the mines. I also worked for a couple of years as a long-distance lorry driver. In 1973, when there was few jobs in this area, I went down to Lancashire looking for work and managed to get a job with the National Coal Board. There were 11 pits in the area at the time. One of them was the Agecroft Colliery in Salford, near Manchester. We used to go from pit to pit collecting old machinery from the pit face and taking it up to the surface for salvage and we also installed new machinery at the pit face.

I had quite a broad Geordie accent at the time, though over 20 years I've lost a bit of it. I was living in a flat in Prestwich and would go for a drink in a local pub after my shift. But most of the time was spent working.

There happened to be a fella who worked at Agecroft who was always playing pranks. He was a big practical joker and he thought it would be a huge joke if he told the police they should speak to me because I was a Geordie living on my own in a flat. He was a nice enough lad, it was just that he was forever playing practical jokes.

In the pits they tried to imitate my accent. Once they heard your voice, there was a certain way they would look at you. When I got the area job, going around all the pits, they would always come out with it. 'Don't you know he's the Ripper', they'd say. It was a big joke to all of them.

I was interviewed by detectives three times. The first time they asked me general questions and they were particularly interested in what I did in my spare time. I told them I went for a drink sometimes. They asked me what pub it was and I told them. All the time I was answering questions, one of the detectives would be writing everything down. The interview went on for a long time.

The detectives were very thorough. In the second interview they wanted to take an impression of my teeth; just the top front teeth. They also asked what blood group I was and, as far as I remember, I was also asked to provide them with a sample of my handwriting, which they wanted to compare with the letters.

The third interview lasted the longest. They covered just about everything. Then one of the detectives said he was going to ask me one question and if I could give him an answer they would eliminate me from the inquiry. He asked me where I was on a certain day two years earlier. Well, I couldn't remember that. They wanted to know where I was between the hours of 6pm and 2am on that particular day. I said, 'You must be joking. How can you expect me to remember that when it was two years ago?'

I was able to tell them that I knew I would have been working that day. I had to go through all my work records to prove it. I was on day shift that day. I told the police that, after work, I would have gone to the local pub at about 7.30pm for a drink. I remember the pub in Prestwich was called the Park Hotel. I would have returned to my flat at about 10.30pm to sleep until my shift the next morning.

But that left a gap between 10.30pm and 2am. And it was this gap that the detectives were concerned about. As I lived on my own in flats where everyone kept themselves to themselves that proved to be the most difficult thing for me. No one saw anyone else coming in or out. No one ever did get back to me to say I was eliminated from the inquiry.

When they came the first time and said, 'We're detectives' it was worrying. There are a million things go through your mind. I wondered if there had been an accident; whether my parents or other relatives were all right. The detectives, who I think were from Manchester, were courteous enough and I did all I could to help them. But it all made me think how innocent people could be blamed for something they hadn't done.

When they came the second time and said they wanted an impression of my teeth, it was even more worrying. I told a couple of lads in the pub about it and they were pretty amazed. I told my family and close friends what was going on, but it wasn't the type of thing to broadcast.

With me working in so many pits, where between something like 600 to 1,000 men were employed, word soon got around. Lots of people would come up to me and ask if I had been interviewed about the Ripper murders. Everyone was convinced he was a Geordie. I got a hell of a lot of stick about it. Whoever sent the tape caused a lot of grief.

Every day the finger was being pointed at me and because I toured round so many pits there were more and more people pointing the finger. I never bore any grudge against the lad who had told police to have a look at me. We worked well together and, in fact, I helped him when he was in a bad accident. We were installing a new gearbox on a piece of machinery at the coal face at the Goldburn Colliery, between Manchester and Liverpool.

What we were doing was lifting it and putting chocks underneath before we would put it on a trolley to take it to the pit face. We were using brand new link chains to lift the gear box, which was very heavy. I was heaving away while my mate was putting the chocks underneath.

As he was putting one of the chocks in place, suddenly the chain slipped and the gear box fell right on to his left hand. He pulled his hand away and his little finger was left there, underneath the machinery. It had been severed and blood was gushing everywhere. I helped him up, and he weighed about 16 stone, and gave him first aid. Then I rushed to get the emergency team down there. There were no thoughts of revenge or grudges in my mind at all.

Even though he had put the police on to me, he was my mate and work colleague. After I moved back to the North East I never heard from him. But I have often wondered what he is doing now and if he's still around. '

Jack the Lorry Driver

John Morris, 51, of Monkwearmouth, Sunderland, was working for Homeworthy Furniture in the town and living in Blyth Street, Town End Farm, at the time of the Ripper murders. He had worked previously as a miner at four pits in the area, Usworth, Castletown, Boldon and Wearmouth. He is married to Valerie and the couple have no children

He says:

‘They questioned a lot of lorry drivers and I think, if I remember rightly, there were about 14 drivers in total working at Homeworthy who were questioned. I was interviewed by the police twice.

The first interview was at my house in Town End Farm and the second, about four months later, was again at the house. I was being questioned voluntarily. I was never arrested. I had to give them a sample of my handwriting. That was done by them dictating a letter to me which I had to write down. They also had a tape recorder and asked me questions so they could tape my voice.

After that they asked me my blood goup, which I know from my Army days was O positive. They didn't ask me to bite on any mould and, come to think of it, there wouldn't have been much point really - in those days I only had about five teeth. The CID men then said I wasn't the one they were looking for.

I lost most of my teeth because of a skiing accident in Austria when I was in the Army. I had signed up for nine years with the Royal Artillery 94 Locating Regiment and we were based in Celle, Germany. It was while I was in the Army that I got my heavy goods vehicle licence. I was 19 when I signed up for the full screw (nine years) but I left after I had a battle with the regimental sergeant major.

Because of my time in the Army, I had lost some of my strong Sunderland accent. It became kind of semi-posh, if you like. I remember I first heard the tape on the wireless when they were on the hunt for Sutcliffe. He sounded a bit of a rough'en and he was definitely from Sunderland.

In about September, 1979, I had driven the lorry down to Leeds to deliver some furniture from Homeworthy to a Wimpey Bar. I had been driving for so long the tacograph reading was high and I had to take a break, so I parked the wagon up in the Chapeltown area of Leeds and tried to get some kip, because I had to be up at 5am the next morning.

There was me, a lorry driver from Sunderland, right in the area where the Ripper was killing women. Looking back I wasn't surprised they wanted to interview me. When they came I just wanted to be helpful, so I answered all their questions as best I could. But it's fair to say I was shaking in my boots. With being on the road and that, it made me sit up and think. ’

Jack the Teacher

John Goymer, of Houghton, near Sunderland, was travelling from Wearside to Leeds during the five years of the Ripper's reign of terror. He was training to be a teacher at the University of Leeds.

‘My story , and why I became the focus of interest by police, really is quite spooky in many ways. In 1975 I went to Leeds University, where I was doing a degree in politics and, later, I did a postgraduate course in Manchester. So I was in the area for five years during the Ripper's activities.

I remember what happened was that I lived in a flat in Houghton, where I'm originally from. I had kept the flat on and was travelling backwards and forwards because my father was quite ill. He just wasn't particularly well at the time.

I was courting Sue, who is now my wife, and when I was at Leeds University I stayed at the students' hall of residence, Boddington Hall. The meals were provided, it was secure and it had all the student facilities. I had a car at the time, a white Ford Cortina, and I would travel along the Otley Road into Leeds every day.

I was interviewed by police both up here and in West Yorkshire. They said they had an interest because of my white car.

Looking back on it now I was travelling from the Sunderland area down to Leeds as a student right throughout the five-year period that Peter Sutcliffe was on the rampage. I know I had nothing whatsoever to do with the murders or the tape but, like everyone else, I was intrigued by the story.

I took it all in a relaxed fashion. To me it was no big deal and I helped the police as much as I could.

In the first interview, police arrived at the student halls of residence in Leeds. It was very low-key and informal. They were interested in me because of the white car. A white car had something to do with the inquiry. It was unusual in those days for a student at university to have a car.

That interview was before the tape was broadcast. I know that because in June and July, 1979, I no longer lived in Leeds. I had been at Leeds University for three years and after my course finished, in 1979, I went on to study for a post graduate certificate in education at the Bolton Institute, which was part of Manchester University, and I was living in Leigh.

I remember that at the college, while I was in teacher training, I was taking a group of pre-police students. I was on 11-weeks teaching practice at the time. I went in one day to take this group for a full hour class and I remember it was quite discursive. There was a lot of discussion going on.

I later learned that one of the men had been taping my voice which was later checked with the tape that was broadcast. He had done that surreptitiously, without my permission. But he didn't know that I had already been interviewed by the police.

The second time I was interviewed by police was at home in Houghton, and this was after the tape was broadcast. I knew I had nothing to do with it so I was as helpful as I could be. They asked me to write a letter, which they dictated, and it contained certain phrases. They also looked at my teeth. I don't have a gap in my teeth. My blood group isn't B either, I'm O positive.

Among my friends and colleagues it was a bit of a joke and a topic of conversation. Up here there were many people that used to remark that I was a suspect. The spooky thing about it was that when Peter Sutcliffe was found it turned out that, facially, we were very similar.

There were many spooky similarities. The facial similarities. The fact that I was travelling to and from that area when these things were going on and the time I spent there; five years which happened to be the five years Peter Sutcliffe was active. And then there was the white Ford Cortina.

Looking back now I'm not surpised that police came out to see me. It was my responsibility to be as helpful as I could be. Now what sometimes annoys me is when I hear about wrongful arrests. It can happen so easily. ’

Jack the Journalist

James (not his real name, he does not wish to be identified) was working as a journalist on the evening newspaper, the Sunderland Echo, when Ripper Squad detectives called into the head office at Pennywell to tell him they wanted to speak to him.

He says:

‘I was at work and I got a message to say there were two policemen to see me. So I went through to the reception and there were two burly coppers who said they were from Leeds. They said they had been told where I was by my mother. I knew they were after the Ripper and the voice experts had pinned the fella who had sent the tape down to the Castletown and Hylton Castle areas.

They were doing house-to-house inquiries and when they called at my old house my mother said she didn't have any sons living with her at the time. Because she told them where I was at the time the big joke around the office was that I had been fingered as the Ripper by my own mother.

When they came here they wanted to have a look at our days off diary. They wanted proof I was working on certain days. This was sent off to the Fraud Squad to sort out.

During the interview I had to read out a statement. I remember it had the word 'definitely' in it and the person who made the tape had a very Wearside way of saying that word. They also wanted me to bite on some kind of mould to get an impression from my teeth and I did what they asked. I was checked out, like everyone else who had links with Castletown or Hylton Castle, and that was it. I was cleared.

It was a big joke and I dined out on it for weeks after that. Whenever I hear the tape it sends a cold shiver down my back. Still today, after nearly 20 years, people say I was grassed by my own mother. I knew I hadn't sent the tape, the police knew I hadn't, and I can say that ... Definitely.’

Jack the Engineer

Fred Stobbart, now aged 58, was 38 at the time of the Ripper inquiry. He is married to Mary with one daughter, Audrey, who was aged ten at the time. Mr Stobbart, from Hetton, near Sunderland, often travelled to West Yorkshire because of his job as an electrical engineer with the firm GEC Elliott Automation.

He says:

'In 1979/1980 I was employed in the service department of GEC Elliott Automation as a senior engineer. One of our regular customers was ICI's Nitram and CCF fertiliser manufacturing plants in Billingham, Teesside. I had been doing work for them on their premises for about ten years before that.

I answered the telephone one day at our services depot in Wallsend and the call was from a detective inspector who said they were wanting to get in touch with a Mr Stobbart who they believed worked for GEC Elliott Automation. He was a little taken aback when I said I was that person.

They told me that my name had been given to them at ICI as a person answering the general description of a man they were looking for in connection with the 'Jack the Ripper' inquiries and asked if they could come to our offices to interview me.

I said that might be a little embarrassing for me and asked if I could go to the police station instead. They agreed and I arranged to attend the police station about an hour later. After he had hung up, I telephoned the police station to confirm there was, in fact, a detective wanting to interview me and I wasn't the victim of a practical joke.

The detectives interviewed me at Wallsend Police Station. They asked me for my whereabouts on various days and I told them I had no idea, but that there would be a record kept at our office. They played the tape of the suspected 'Ripper' to me and I told them that, in my view, the person on the tape came from Castletown, North Hylton, or thereabouts.

About ten days later I went to ICI again to be met by shouts of: 'Here's Fred, the Ripper'. I wasn't put out by this and joined in the fun. However, on seeing me, one of the tiffys (an artificer) made a hasty exit from the workshop in a barrage of jeers and laughter from his colleagues. In fact in the next year or so this tiffy avoided me like the plague. Eventually, I decided, to prevent any further embarrassment for him, I would draw the matter to a close.

I arranged to visit ICI whilst the tiffys were in their workshop. I sauntered up to the workshop with THE tiffy inside and then I leaned up against the door so that he could not easily escape while I talked to an electrician in a lighthearted way about 'Jack the Ripper' and how I'd been pulled in for questioning.

This seemed to do the trick and after that he no longer ran away, although neither did he seek my company. Years later, and even now, if ever I meet some of the people from ICI, they still call me 'Fred the Ripper'.

I wasn't bothered about being interviewed and the detectives were perfectly nice about it. I wasn't worried and I did everything I could to assist the police, who, after all, were only doing their job.

I was happy to do it because police were after somebody out there who was murdering women. He could have murdered my children. The man who sent the tape is as bloody guilty as the Ripper. He must have been a half-wit.

I don't think they'll ever catch him now because the trail has gone so cold and people do lose their memories. But if they do catch him he wants stringing up. '

Jack the Detective

Detective Constable George Virtue was one of the Ripper Squad on the trail of Wearside Jack. That did not stop him from being interviewed as a potential suspect. He was eliminated because he was able to tell investigating officers he happened to be working on another murder case when the Yorkshire Ripper killed one of his victims.

He says:

'I was born in Pallion and I was interviewed myself. I was interviewed because all the reports went down to Yorkshire and a police officer down there thought my handwriting was similar to that in the letters and someone said my voice sounded like that on the tape.

I was interviewed three times but I wasn't bothered at all. I just wanted to help as best I could. I was eliminated from the inquiry because I had been working on a murder inquiry in Blyth, Northumberland, at the time one of the Ripper murders took place. I remember the victim in Blyth was a chemist who was stabbed during a burglary. '

Jack the Welfare Worker

Gordon Lilley, 74, who is married with two grown-up daughters, has lived all his life in Castletown and was an independent councillor for the village for several years. At the time of the Ripper inquiry he was a social welfare worker for British Coal.

He says:

'We were as flabbergasted as anyone else when they came to interview me, for various reasons really. I was a prominent local councillor and if anyone got to know I was being interviewed they may have thought there was something afoot. Being a local lad I wasn't worried that much because there were hundreds of other people interviewed in Castletown.

There was no doubt about it, from the word go, that the man was from this area of the world because of his local dialect.

At the time I was working for the Coal Industry's Social Welfare Organisation, covering the pits at Herrington, Ryhope, Silksworth, Tunstall, Castletown, Offerton and at Boldon. Most were pit villages. I was first employed by the Coal Board as a manager's clerk, before I became a social welfare officer.

What we did was organise social activities for the miners during their time off work and we arranged all sorts of things; whippet racing, bowls, football, cricket, to name just a few. We did a lot of youth welfare work as well with the apprentices, organising climbing, camping and orienteering activities.

One of the highlights of the job, for me, was my involvement with the apprentices in the Duke of Edinburgh Award Scheme, which was a privilege to work for in itself, but in the mid-1970s I had to take 30 apprentices down to St James' Palace to be presented with their awards. I was introduced to Prince Philip and I shook his hand.

In 1979, when we all heard the tape for the first time, I thought nothing about it, only that it sounded like someone from Sunderland - until there was a knock on my door, that is. I am not sure if it was a sergeant or a constable that wanted to speak to me, but I know it was a local police officer. He said they were making local inquiries and there was nothing for me to worry about. He was quite friendly, there was nothing brusque about his attitude. In fact we had a joke or two.

We had young girls at the time and the murders were something we were worried about. One of our girls was married and had left home and the other, as far as I can recall, was in the process of being married.

The police officer referred to various things that had been in the papers and he played the tape and asked me for my views on the matter. The word 'weird' comes into it. Being a former councillor I had to be careful what I said. Part of the interview was about my blood group, which was probably one of the reasons they wanted to interview me. I am of the B blood group.

The family and a few people around the doors knew about it. I didn't go out of my way to tell people about the interview, though I think I did joke about it at work. ’

Jack the Councillor

Councillor Les Mann, who has served Sunderland Council for years, representing Castletown, was interviewed by Ripper Squad detectives because he and his wife sometimes took caravan holidays in Yorkshire.

He says:

‘I remember sitting in here listening to the radio and hearing the tape for the first time. It was definitely a Geordie or Sunderland voice but I always thought there was a bit of a Welsh lilt to it. The voice experts pinpointed Sunderland and then Castletown and that's where the police concentrated their inquiries. All the men in the village were interviewed.

I remember there was one lad who lived in the same street as me who worked away a lot of the time. Somebody told the police they thought it was him and he was questioned but eliminated.

Of course the police were interested in talking to people who visited Yorkshire and as it happened we had a little caravan at the time and used to visit North Yorkshire regularly. Word about that somehow got back to the police and I remember sitting here one Saturday morning and there was a knock on the door. It was a police officer.

He was quite a big lad. Anyway, I offered him a cup of tea and he told me that I'd better make one for his mate as well who was at the back door. So there was him at the front, his mate at the back, and two others sitting in a van outside.

They came in and played the tape and then they asked me to write on a sheet of paper something they were going to tell me to write. That letter was taken away and obviously compared to the writing in one of the letters.

The tape did sound like someone from Sunderland. The thing is there's a difference in the accents or dialects of people living close to each other. People in Hetton, say, sound different from people in Castletown and in Hendon. ’

Jack the Cockney

Charles Telling, 47, who lives with his wife, Carol, in Doxford Park, Sunderland, was never interviewed by Ripper Squad detectives but they took a keen interest in him and questioned his relatives - Carol's parents - who lived in Hylton Castle. Mr Telling says the police interest in him showed one of two things; they were either very thorough or were clutching at straws. He says this because his accent is nothing like a Sunderland accent - he was born within spitting distance of the Bow Bells in London's East End.

He says:

‘When the tape first came out, from what I could gather, the police were carrying out house-to-house inquiries in the Hylton Castle area. Carol's from Hylton Castle. She used to work at Thorn Electronics but was made redundant when they started making colour tellys and the unions were asking for more pay.

Carol went to work at Aldermaston and she was living in a hostel which was provided for the workers. I was working at the Lansing Bagnal factory but I was staying at the hostel. Outsiders, or those who worked 'behind the wire', as we used to say, were allowed to live in the hostel but had to pay full rent. That's where Carol and I met.

We got together and got married in 1976 and bought a house in Basingstoke. We were still working. With Carol being from this area we used to come up to Sunderland regularly, travelling through Yorkshire. Both my parents are dead so we used to take every opportunity to come up to the North East.

When they were doing the house-to-house inquiries, they called at Carol's parents who told them Carol and I regularly travelled through Yorkshire. I was told the police were very, very interested. They took a look at our wedding photograph, which was on the mantelpiece. But it was when they were told I had a Cockney accent that they decided I needn't be interviewed.

This wedding photograph of Charles and Carol Telling, was on the mantelpiece at Carol's parents' home in Hylton Castle, Sunderland. Ripper Squad police were interested in speaking to Mr Telling and examined the photo but eliminated him from inquiries when they discovered he is a "true" Cockney.
Picture: *Charles and Carol Telling.*

"I was born in Bow, East London, within hearing distance of Bow Bells, so, in that respect, I'm a true Cockney. With the police showing an interest in me at the time it shows how much they were clutching at straws and just how wide the inquiry was. '

Jack the Electrician

Two relatives of Syliva Goss, 56, of Southwick, Sunderland, were interviewed by Ripper police. One was her husband, Arthur, an electrician at Wearmouth Colliery, who has since died, and the other was one of her brothers, Trevor, who had moved from Sunderland to Halifax where he was working as a painter and decorator.

Sylvia Goss, of Southwick, Sunderland, whose husband, Arthur, a colliery electrician, and brother, Trevor, a painter and decorator, were both interviewed in the Ripper inquiry.
Picture: *Patrick Lavelle.*

Mrs Goss says:

'We were living in a four-bedroomed colliery house in Wreath Quay Road, Monkwearmouth, at the time. Arthur was a maintenance electrician at Wearmouth Colliery and I was working at the Pyrex factory in Deptford. Arthur had been in the Army for nine years and he got the job at the pit when we moved back here.

When the police came to my house, they wanted to take a sample of Arthur's handwriting and they were asking where he was on certain dates. He had kept a diary from his Army days and he still used it at the colliery, so he was able to tell them where he was.

The second time they came, they wanted to know what his shoe size was and what type of shoes he wore. He took a size nine. I don't know if they had found a footprint or not. As for his accent, well, we used to call Arthur the Cockey Geordie because he had lost his Sunderland accent when he was in the Army. His dialect was a bit of a mixture.

The police asked me if I had any other relatives in the area. I come from a big family, with six brothers and seven sisters. I told them I had a brother called Arthur who lived in Blyth, Northumberland, but they already seemed to know all about it. They must have been doing some checking before they came.

I had another brother, Trevor, who lived in Halifax. He moved down to Halifax on the day he was married. His wife, Mary, used to live in Plains Farm, Sunderland, and her dad lived in Halifax. She wanted to be near her dad and Trevor was looking for work, and there was no work in Sunderland at the time. They're divorced now.

He started working as a painter and decorator. What with him having a Wearside accent and living and working in Yorkshire, he was also questioned by police. They were making inquiries into all the people from Sunderland who were living in the area. He used to tell me he was forever being taken off the job by the police.

When I got to know Trevor had been interviewed I thought, fair enough, he's from Sunderland and he was living in Halifax. But when they interviewed my husband I thought, 'What have you got to do with it?'. I asked my sisters if any of their men had been interviewed and they said no. It was probably because Arthur had a beard. It turned out he had a slight resemblance to Peter Sutcliffe, but only because of the beard. When Arthur first heard the tape he said, 'Don't say owt you are thinking. Keep it to yourself'. He said he sounded like a lad he knew, but we couldn't say things like that. Arthur was very careful about what he said, what with him having been in the forces.'

Jack the Pervert

Christine (not her real name, she can't be named for legal reasons) was living with her boyfriend in Pallion, Sunderland, when he was interviewed by Ripper Squad detectives. Her boyfriend was hiding a dark secret from her - he was a convicted sex offender. Police interviewed her partner because of his previous sex crimes, but they always told Christine their inquiries were "just routine".

A year later Christine married her partner and they had a child. She says she would never have married him if she had known he was a pervert. She discovered his sordid past when he appeared in court on yet another sex offence and after he suddenly changed his plea to guilty. Up until the sudden guilty plea, and not knowing his criminal history, Christine had believed in her huband's innocence. But all was revealed when his antecedents were read out at Newcastle Crown Court.

Christine says:

'Before we were married we were living in Pallion, Sunderland, and the police came and they said they wanted to interview him about the Yorkshire Ripper killings. They told me that they were doing house-to-house inquiries and that their questioning was just routine. They said it was 'only routine' fairly often.

I was quite cool about it but I remember having a feeling that there was something not right about it and that it wasn't just a routine inquiry. They interviewed him at the house and I wanted to be present. I wanted to know what was going on.

One of the reasons he was interviewed was that he was a sales rep at the time and he travelled all over the country, including West Yorkshire. But it was only much later that I found out the main reason for the interview - he was a convicted pervert.

We lived together for about a year and then we got married. But if I had known he had convictions for indecency on women I would have never married him in the first place. When I did find out about his criminal record, which was long after the interview, that was it. I filed for divorce.

These days people have a right to know if sex offenders are living in their community. But then even the wives of sex offenders had no right to be told of their records. Now, to think that this

The Yorkshire Ripper, Peter Sutcliffe, thought this was one of the best pictures he had of himself. He gave copies of this picture to many of his women visitors and "penpals", among them Olive Curry, of North Shields. **Picture: The Northern Echo.**

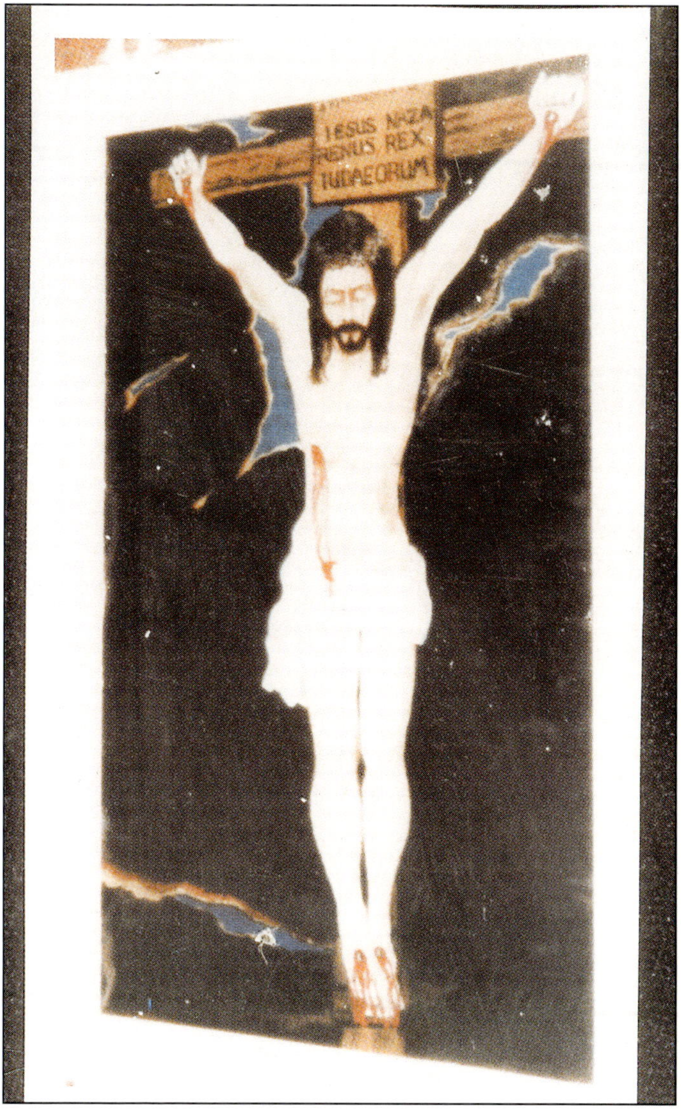

Peter Sutcliffe painted this picture of The Crucifixion and appears to have used an image of his own face rather than that of Christ. The painting hangs on a wall in Broadmoor Hospital, Berkshire. Sutcliffe would only send pictures of the painting to his closest friends, among them Olive Curry. **Picture: The Northern Echo.**

Semi-professional singer and talented artist John Gaffney, of Sunderland, with some of the hundreds of sketches he drew on beer mats while touring pubs and clubs in the North East. Hundreds of the sketches were examined by Ripper Squad police in the hunt for Wearside Jack. **Picture: Patrick Lavelle.**

Local singer and artist John Gaffney sketched hundreds of people on beer mats in pubs and clubs around the North East in the 1970s. Some of his subjects knew they were being sketched, others did not, and none knew that the beer mats were taken away by Ripper Squad police to examine in their hunt for Wearside Jack/the Yorkshire Ripper. With Mr Gaffney's permission, many of the sketches are featured over the next few pages. Do you recognise any of the faces?

Do you recognise any of these faces?

Do you recognise any of these faces?

Do you recognise any of these faces?

Do you recognise any of these faces?

Do you recognise any of these faces?

Do you recognise any of these faces?

Do you recognise any of these faces?

Do you recognise any of these faces?

Do you recognise any of these faces?

Do you recognise any of these faces?

Do you recognise any of these faces?

Do you recognise any of these faces?

Do you recognise any of these faces?

Ron Fulbirg, of Sunderland - "Jack the Coalman" - was arrested and questioned 14 times by Ripper Squad detectives. He says he has yet to be eliminated from inquiries and has yet to have material returned to him taken from his house in Bradford, including a hammer, for forensic examination. **Picture: The Sunderland Echo.**

John Morris, of Sunderland - "Jack the Lorry Driver" - was twice questioned by Ripper Squad detectives. He was not asked to bite on a mould to see if he had a gap in his teeth like other "suspects". Mr Morris says he only had five teeth at the time. **Picture: The Sunderland Echo**.

Ken McKone, of Seaham, County Durham - "Jack the Pitman" - who was interviewed three times by detectives from Manchester hunting the Yorkshire Ripper. Mr McKone lived and worked in Preston at the time of the Ripper murders. **Picture: Patrick Lavelle.**

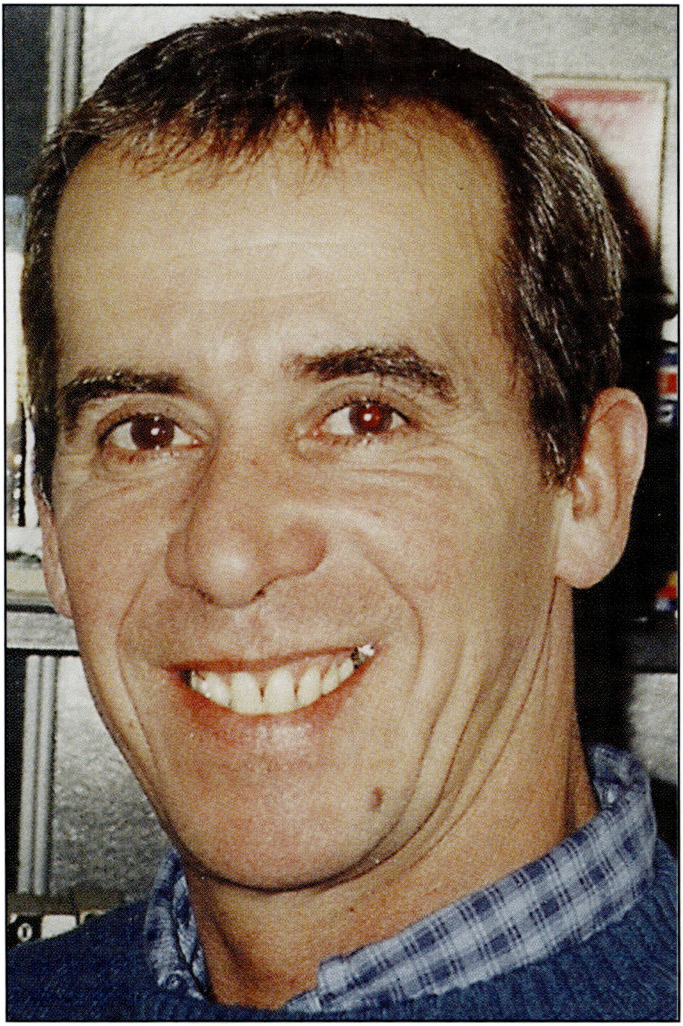

Peter Robson - "Jack the Shopfitter" - of Houghton. He was working in Manchester at the time of the Ripper killings and was interviewed twice by detectives - once on the hard shoulder of the M62 when his car broke down shortly after leaving the city. He was interviewed the second time in Sunderland, in view of hundreds of shoppers. **Picture: Patrick Lavelle.**

Charles Telling, of Doxford Park, Sunderland - "Jack the Cockney". Although never interviewed by police, they took a keen interest in Mr Telling as he regularly travelled through Yorkshire to see his wife, Carol's, parents in Hylton Castle, Sunderland. **Picture: Patrick Lavelle.**

The late Arthur Goss - "Jack the Electrician" - who was interviewed at his home in Monkwearmouth. He was one of two relatives of Sylvia Goss interviewed by police. **Picture: Courtesy of Sylvia Goss.**

John Goymer - "Jack the Teacher" - of Houghton. He was twice interviewed by Ripper Squad detectives. A police officer he was teaching in Leeds also secretly taped his voice. His resemblance to Peter Sutcliffe, says Mr Goymer, was one of the "spooky" things about his story. **Picture: John Goymer.**

Gordon Lilley - "Jack the Welfare Worker" - of Castletown, Sunderland. The former prominent village councillor was interviewed at his home and had to give police a sample of his handwriting. He helped all he could - the Ripper needed to be caught. **Picture: Patrick Lavelle.**

man was touching my body, makes me feel dirty and it makes me feel angry. Thinking about it makes my skin crawl.

I remember how cool he was about the interview but I was in a terrible state.

It was in 1984 or 1985 that I finally found out the truth. He was up in court for indecent assault but he was denying it. Not knowing anything about his sordid past I believed he was innocent. Then, suddenly, he changed his plea to guilty and his antecedent history came out. He had been convicted of sex offences since the age of 17. I remember that day as if it was yesterday because my whole world fell apart.

To me all that was abhorrent. I was just so shocked and I knew I would get a divorce. It didn't take long for the divorce to come through. I remember thinking I wanted him to be hurt, physically hurt, maimed for life.

Now, whenever I hear anything on the news or read anything in the newspapers about the Ripper inquiry and the tape, it all comes flooding back. If only the police had told me in 1979 or 1980 the real reason why he was being interviewed all my heartache could have been avoided, because I would have ditched him there and then. ’

Jack the Shopfitter

Peter Robson, 48, of Houghton, near Sunderland, was working in Manchester at the time of the Ripper murders. He was refitting a take-way shop in Manchester's Piccadilly, working alongside three other men from Sunderland. Mr Robson was interviewed twice by Ripper Squad detectives. And a barmaid in a pub in Manchester refused to serve him after hearing his broad Wearside accent, and deciding he must be the Ripper.

Mr Robson says:

‘We were fitting out this Kwix Snack Bar just off Manchester's Piccadilly and me and the other lads were living in digs in Manchester and travelling back home every weekend. I do have a brother in Castletown but I think the police were interested in me because of all the travelling I did.

I was born and bred in Sunderland. We used to live at the old Farm House in Thorney Close. It's pulled down now.

I was working as an electrician and the businessman we were working for had won the franchise to fit out 33 shops across the country. They were Kwix Snack Bars, Wimpey Bars and other types of take-away. We worked in Burnley, Leeds and other places, as well as Manchester.

The jobs lasted a couple of weeks. They were doing trade during the day and were busy so we were doing as much re-fitting as we could during the night. We used to pride ourselves on getting the job done as quickly as we could, so there was as little loss of business for the shop as possible. It was hard work but we were handsomely paid.

I had worked as a miner before that, in Vane Tempest Colliery at Seaham. I wanted to get out fast.

The first thing that happened to me was quite strange. What we used to do was work throughout the night but we usually nipped out at about 9.30pm to catch the last hour in the pub and then we would go back to work. We used to go in this one bar for a drink, it was called The Shakespeare.

There was one particular night we went in. We were all in work clothes and I had some of my tools with me. I might have had a screwdriver in my pocket. I asked the barmaid for a pint and she said, 'You lot are from up north aren't you' and we told her we were working in the city centre. Then she looked at me and said, 'I'm not serving you. You're the Ripper'. Of course we all just burst out laughing. But she was deadly serious, she wouldn't serve me. One of the other lads had to get my drink in.

There was one weekend when we were travelling back to Sunderland after doing a ghostie - that means working throughout the night to get an early start. We left Manchester between 11am and noon in my mate's old Austin Maxi which was forever overheating and we broke down on the M62 just outside of Manchester. It was an afternoon and all four of us were in the car. One of us went over to the SOS 'phone to try to get a recovery truck to come out. We just sat in the car waiting.

We waited for about three hours. There was no sign of a recovery truck. But then a car pulled up in front of us and two men got out. One of them was wearing a traditional raincoat with his belt hanging at the back. They just looked like typical detectives and it turned out that's what they were. They told us they were police working on the Yorkshire Ripper case.

We all got interviewed. I was interviewed in the back of the car. He asked me who I was, where I was working, where I was going, my name, my address, my height, my weight. I said, 'Would you like to know the size of my dick?' They wanted to know everything about us. After the interviews they left and then we sat waiting for the recovery truck, which turned up eventually.

I didn't think much more of it, really. After the Manchester job we came back to Sunderland and we started work fitting-out what was then the Biz Bar in Park Lane. We were converting it into a burger bar. It's now Johnnie Ringo's and whenever I walk past the place appears to be dimly lit. But, when we were working on it, it was bright and, what with the massive display window at the front, everyone passing could see us at work.

One day I was up the ladders working on the ceiling lighting and I heard one of my mates shout, 'Pete, they're coming to get you'. I looked down and there were two detectives who said they wanted to talk to me. Well, my mates thought it was a big laugh. They started shouting things like, 'We grassed you up' and, 'We've got the reward money spent already'. I think the reward for catching the Ripper was about £25,000 at the time.

One of the detectives said, 'Are you Peter Robson?' I said I was and he said they wanted to talk to me about a case they were working on. We sat down at a table right in front of the big window at the front of the shop. Hundreds of people were walking past but, thankfully, I did have my back to the window.

They asked me to write something down from a statement, which one of them dictated, and they gave me a sheet of paper. I was told to just do my normal handwriting and I think I filled about half the page. I can't remember exactly what it was they told me to write down. I was a bit nervous about it and I was over the moon when it was over and done with. I never heard back from them.

The four of us who were interviewed that day on the M62 were all working in the Biz Bar at the time. But I was the only one interviewed a second time. I don't know why. I did feel a little uncomfortable but the police were only doing their job and they had to find this killer who was still at large.

There were quite a few people who knew I had been interviewed. I have never been in trouble with the police in my life. Looking back on it now, me getting interviewed twice by police for the Ripper murders was my little claim to infamy.

I know they still haven't caught the man who sent the tape. If he's still alive he should be caught. After all, with us coming up to the Millennium, this is the day and age to settle old debts.'

Jack the Newsagent

The Sunderland Ripper Squad officers followed up every lead in their hunt for Wearside Jack/the Yorkshire Ripper, however remote the possibility that the information obtained would lead them to their man. Information from a source in Nottingham resulted in three detectives calling on Jack Jacques in Newbottle, near Sunderland. Jack was probably the most unlikely "suspect" in the whole inquiry ... he was aged 73 at the time.

Jack, in 1999 aged 93, recalls his interview:

'I used to work in the Co-op in Newbottle and when I retired I took over a newsagents in the village. One day there was a knock on my door and when I went to answer there were three detectives standing there. They told me what they wanted and after looking me up and down one of them turned to the other two and said, 'I think we must have the wrong door' and he started laughing.

I invited them in and one of them said that they had some information from someone in Nottingham who had told police that my voice sounded like that on the tape. I was amazed. One of the detectives said he obviously didn't think it was me but they would have to interview me anyway and fill out a report.

Jack Jacques, of Newbottle, near Sunderland, was probably the most unlikely "suspect" in the hunt for Wearside Jack/the Yorkshire Ripper. He was aged 73 at the time. Picture: *Patrick Lavelle.*

When they mentioned Nottingham I could only think of my days in the Army. I was stationed at the biggest stores depot in the world, near Nottingham. There were civilians working there as well.

All I could think was that someone I had met there, all those years ago, had remembered my accent and decided to call the police.

I wasn't worried about it, in fact I laughed. The police officers were also laughing about it. But they still had to ask me a few questions and do their report. They had a job to do.'

Jack the Foreman

Dad-of-two Clive Parker, 53, was working for the Port of Sunderland Authority at the time of the Ripper killings. He provided a detective with a sample of his handwriting; a love letter he had written to his wife Brenda. Police also took away a shoe for forensic examination.

Clive, of Washington, says:

'I worked for the River Wear Commissioners which became the Port of Sunderland Authority after I had been in the Merchant Navy for ten years. My wife and I lived in Fulwell, Sunderland, at the time and our son Jonathan would have been five and Susan, our daughter, would have been aged about ten.

As a foreman fitter at the port I was in charge of mechanical engineering repairs in the whole of the docks complex. That included working on cranes, dock gates, coal staithes, conveyors, swing bridges, forklift trucks; anything in the docks that was mechanical.

The police interviewed me at home. They said they were interviewing men of a certain age with a certain shoe size. The detective also said that there were certain times of certain days when I wasn't contactable. I had a pocket radio for work but at the docks I covered miles. I could be away from the port offices for hours at a time.

The detective asked for a sample of my handwriting, so I gave him a letter that I had written to my wife when I was at sea. He didn't ask me to write anything down there and then. I think he was interested in the way I formed the letter L.

He also took one of my shoes away. It was one of a pair of slip-on shoes, I can't remember if it was the left or the right. I got the shoe back but the letter was never returned.

He was also interested in the fact that Brenda and I travelled occasionally to West Yorkshire. At the time my wife was running a little market stall and we used to go to the Leeds and Bradford area to buy wholesale jewellery and children's toys. The car we had at the time was a Renault 9 and we travelled to Leeds or Bradford about once a month because we thought that was the best area in which to buy that type of thing.

Brenda sold the jewellery and toys at car boot sales. There was one we used to go to at the old Thorn's Electricals site at Pallion, another at the greyhound stadium, off Newcastle Road, and another at Sedgefield Racecourse.

The detective asked Brenda how she knew I wasn't the Ripper. I thought it was a huge joke. I thought they were treating this tape with far more seriousness than it warranted. He could have come into my house and heard me say five words and he would have known I wasn't the person who sent the tape. There seemed to be an air of desperation about the whole thing.'

Clive and Brenda Parker at their home in Washington. Brenda says a Ripper Squad detective was interested in talking to them about their love life. Picture: *Patrick Lavelle.*

Brenda says: "They seemed to know so much about Clive before they came here. To me it seemed as if they were implying that Clive might have been the type of man to use prostitutes. The detective also wanted to know about our sex life. I felt insulted and I felt as if our privacy had been intruded upon. I was also angry that they had taken away what was a love letter. I didn't know how many people were going to read the letter, which was private, but I didn't want a lot of people reading details about our personal life."

CHAPTER ELEVEN

Was Jack a Cop?

From the day the hoax tape arrived at Gill Bridge Police Station in Sunderland up until long after the arrest of the Yorkshire Ripper, rumours, speculation and even accusations persisted that the hoaxer of the century was a retired police officer with a grudge or a serving officer unhappy at how the Ripper inquiry was handled.

But those suspicions emerged even before the hoax letters and tape were sent to police, because of the lack of forensic evidence at any of the early murder scenes. As Jack said in one of his letters, there were never any clues for police to follow. The murder scenes were, as he put it, always "as clean as a whistle".

Normally, in such brutal attacks as the Ripper murders, the killer would have been expected to leave some forensic evidence, however minute. Even detectives investigating the murders had suspicions that the killer might have been "in the job".

Police officers in the major incident room at Sunderland's Gill Bridge Police Station dealing with the hundreds of calls from people who believed they knew the voice of Wearside Jack. But even police officers found themselves under suspicion in the massive inquiry. Picture: *The Sunderland Echo.*

After the hoax, the massive inquiry was bound to lead to some police officers being interviewed; those that were would have fitted the general profile of the hoaxer. Many Sunderland police officers came under suspicion.

One officer recalls the day the tape arrived at Gill Bridge. He says: "Several officers gathered around to hear it and some, straight away, turned around and pointed at one policeman and said, 'It's him'. It was only said as a joke, but the thing is, it did sound like him, and many other men in Sunderland."

Another Ripper Squad officer, a detective who does not wish to be named, says it wasn't just the lack of forensic at the murder scenes that led to suspicions that Jack was among their ranks. In the hoax letters the word "uniform" was used rather than "uniformed". He says: "That's a job word. Civilians would normally use the word 'uniformed'.

"Because of that suspicion, a team of six detectives was ordered to look through police pocket books, comparing the handwriting with that of the letters. At the time, police pocket books had to be kept for seven years. This team spent weeks looking at the pocket books of almost all police officers in Sunderland."

The massive inquiry had more ramifications on serving police officers than just the hoaxer suspicions. A number of officers, according to former Ripper Squad detectives, were discovered - by their own wives - to have been using prostitutes. The revelations caused much marital strife and, possibly, marriage breakdowns.

In West Yorkshire, police spent a lot of time talking to prostitutes in the red light areas of Manchester, Bradford, Leeds, Preston and elsewhere. Detectives were particularly interested in any kinky clients the working girls had knowledge of.

One detective says: "There was one bloke who they called the pissy man, because he would pay one of the girls to urinate all over him, while he lay on the floor. There was another who they laughingly called the banana man, because he had extreme curvature of the penis. They had some very weird men as clients."

Another Ripper Squad detective says: "At the West Yorkshire end police were conducting what we term 'three area sightings'. This involved officers keeping observations in one area, then another, then a third. They were all areas where prostitutes walked the streets.

"If they spotted a kerb crawler in one area, they would jot down the make and model of the car, and the registration number, but take no action. If the same car was spotted in the second area they would do the same. But if was seen in the third area - the 'third area sighting' - then the police would call at that person's house.

A newsagent in Sunderland hands one of the thousands of four-page newsletters produced by West Yorkshire Police to a customer in her shop. The newsletters contained details of all the Ripper killings and clues to his identity, including an example of handwriting from one of the Wearside Jack letters. Picture: *The Sunderland Echo.*

"The person would be asked what they were doing in the red light areas and they would have to be eliminated from the inquiry. I can tell you there were quite a few police officers visited at home, many of them married, and there were embarrassed faces all round."

Despite a lot of police officers being interviewed as suspects in the Ripper inquiry - one was only eliminated because he could prove he was working on another murder inquiry at the time of a Ripper killing - speculation still persisted that Jack could be a cop.

In January, 1987, six years after Peter Sutcliffe was arrested but with the hoaxer still at large, a report in the Sunday Express claimed the tape was sent by a police officer "as a joke" in protest at what he thought was the mishandling of the case by George Oldfield.

According to the newspaper report, other police officers were also thought to have known what was going on but did not think the tape would be taken seriously. The allegations, said the Express, were made by a former policeman who, at one time, was a member of Leeds CID.

Later, however, the Deputy Chief Constable of West Yorkshire Police, Mr David Wilmot, said the claims in the Sunday Express were "completely erroneous and irresponsible".

That claim, and more speculation that Jack was a cop, led to an in-depth, two-month inquiry by police, which ended in April, 1987, to test the claims. The inquiry was headed by Superintendent Tony Fitzgerald, of North Yorkshire Police. He found nothing to support the theory.

Later that month, newspapers reported that the claim that Jack was a police officer was made by Ron Smith, a former police officer himself, who was the father of nurse Helen Smith, who had plunged to her death from a hotel balcony in Saudi Arabia. It appeared Mr Smith was disgruntled at the handling of the police investigation into the death of his daughter.

Speculation that Jack was a cop continues, but there has never been any firm evidence to substantiate the claim, which many police officers believe was spread by anti-police activists and fuelled by the vivid imaginations of conspiracy theorists. The "lie" will only be firmly nailed if and when Wearside Jack is caught.

CHAPTER TWELVE

True Crime

The Sunderland Ripper Squad left no stone unturned in its hunt for Wearside Jack. Thousands of items of post had been examined at the town's main sorting office in West Sunniside. Many thousands of men had been tracked down through the registers of births, deaths and marriages at Sunderland's Civic Centre. Information on hundreds of other "suspects" had been obtained from the Department of Health and Social Security complex in Longbenton, North Tyneside.

The tape had been played to thousands of miners at collieries across the North East. Thousands of men had provided samples of their handwriting. Several experts in linguistics had analysed the voice of Jack. Thousands of samples of saliva had been analysed by forensic scientists. Scores of speech therapists across the North East who may have counselled Jack to rid him of his speech impediment had been contacted. Scores of haulage firms employing lorry drivers had had work records checked. Detectives had even examined sketches drawn by local artist John Gaffney on beer mats in North East pubs and clubs.

Was there any other possible lead that could point detectives in the direction of the hoaxer of the century? One police officer thought there was one avenue which had yet to be tested ... the records held at Sunderland's central library in Borough Road on readers with a keen interest in true crime.

The records were examined closely and detectives kept coming across the same name, S. Smith, who lived on the Red House estate in the town. It appeared S. Smith was taking up to four true crime books on loan every week from the central library and, over the years, S. Smith must have read hundreds of books in the genre.

Why was S. Smith so interested in the often macabre and gory details of serial killings, mutilations, rape, murder and mayhem in the pages of true crime books? Ripper Squad detectives decided to pay S. Smith a visit.

Sarah Smith, 68, known as Sadie, was home at the time but her husband, Stan, was at work. Stan was a bus driver and had worked on the buses for 28 years.

Mrs Smith says: "There were two plain clothed detectives. One of them said they wanted to speak to Mr Smith and I told him he was out at work. They asked to come in. So I let them in and I asked what they wanted to talk to Stan about.

"They said they were looking into the tape of the Yorkshire Ripper and wanted to eliminate certain men from the inquiry. They said, 'Your husband doesn't come from Sunderland,' and I said they were right, he came from Birtley.

"They asked what my husband did in his spare time, and I told them he was interested in motorbikes and that we used to travel around a lot, with me riding pillion and sometimes even driving the bike myself. We travelled to Scotland sometimes, and to Yorkshire.

"They seemed to be interested in talking to Stan. I asked them again why they were so interested in my husband. One of them said they were exploring every avenue possible and they had been going through the records in the library picking out the names of those who took out true crime books.

Sadie Smith at her home in Red House, Sunderland, where she still reads true crime books she borrows from Sunderland's central library. Picture: *Patrick Lavelle.*

"I just said, 'That's not Stan! It's me!' And I told them it takes Stan all his time to read the front page of the Echo. They asked me why I was so interested in that type of book and I told them I had always been interested in reading true crime, from the age of 19 when I read the memoirs of Sir Bernard Spilsbury. After I read that book, I was hitched."

Mrs Smith, who has lived in Red House for 33 years, said Stan, who died in 1998, was "never a reader". She says: "I was never worried about them coming to see Stan, because there were thousands of men interviewed by the police.

"They took a sample of his handwriting and they also wanted a sample of my handwriting, which I gave them. The fact that police had looked through the library records just shows they were looking at any and every possibility."

Mrs Smith adds: "It's the true element of the books that attracts me. I'm not really interested in the gory details of murders. I'm more interested in how detectives go about solving the crimes; what clues they follow and how they catch them. The subject has always fascinated me.

"Over the years I've read hundreds of true crime books. I've read books about Jack the Ripper, Mary Ann Cotton, Dr Crippin, Mary Bell, the Bulger case. I've just finished a book about Fred and Rose West. The gory details don't frighten me."

The police inquiry had encompassed so many aspects of the everyday life of people in Sunderland, from the books they read to their work, habits, hobbies and even their sex lives, that it was difficult to fathom how Wearside Jack/the Yorkshire Ripper, was never caught in the earlier stages on the massive police hunt.

The inquiry had an impact in neighbouring County Durham, too, where Chief Constable Arthur Pickering blamed a fall of three per cent in the crime detection rate on the bogus tape and letters. Six officers from Durham's crime support unit had been drafted in to the Ripper inquiry.

Then, in January, 1981, came the breakthrough police had been waiting for - an arrest. But was the suspected serial killer the man who had sent the tape and letters? It was not. It was Bradford lorry driver Peter William Sutcliffe, who had no real links with Sunderland. His arrest, however, was greeted with a huge sigh of relief both in West Yorkshire and on Wearside.

IMPORTANT DATES IN THE HUNT FOR WEARSIDE JACK

November 20, 1975	• **The battered body of mother-of-two Joan Harrison, 26, lies in a derelict lock-up garage in the Avenham area of Preston.**
January 21, 1978	• **Ripper victim Yvonne Pearson, 22, is killed in Bradford.**
March 8, 1978	• **Wearside Jack posts his first hoax letter in Sunderland but, according to a Ripper Squad detective, he fails to mention the murder of Yvonne Pearson, whose body has yet to be discovered.**
March 13, 1978	• **Jack posts his second hoax letter in Sunderland.**
May 16, 1978	• **Vera Millward, 41, presumed to be the Ripper's tenth victim (she was the ninth) is killed in Manchester.**
March 23, 1979	• **Wearside Jack sends his third hoax letter to George Oldfield and, according to a detective, mentions how Vera Millward told him about having treatment at a local hospital.**
April 4, 1979	• **Student Josephine Whitaker, 19, is killed by the Ripper on playing fields in Halifax.**
June, 1979	• **Jack sends the hoax tape to George Oldfield.**
June 26, 1979	• **The tape is broadcast nationally and the Ripper hunt switches to Wearside.**
September 2, 1979	• **The Ripper kills 20-year-old student Barbara Leach in Bradford.**
August 18, 1980	• **The Ripper kills Marguerite Walls, 47, in Farsley.**
November 17, 1980	• **Student Jacqueline Hill is killed by the Ripper in Leeds.**
January 2, 1981	• **Peter Sutcliffe is arrested in Sheffield.**

PART THREE

Who Was Wearside Jack?

CHAPTER THIRTEEN

The Arrest of the Yorkshire Ripper

Peter William Sutcliffe was arrested by police on routine patrol in Sheffield on January 2, 1981, and on the 5th of that month he appeared before magistrates in Dewsbury charged with the murder of Leeds student Jacqueline Hill. Later, in April, the 34-year-old Bradford lorry driver appeared at the Old Bailey and pleaded guilty to the manslaughter of 13 women in the North of England and the attempted murder of seven others between 1975 and 1980. One killing not included when pleas were taken was that of Joan Harrison in Preston in 1975.

The judge in the Ripper trial, Mr Justice Boreham. Picture: *The Sunderland Echo.*

At his trial, Sutcliffe told the jury he had friends with Wearside accents and that he used to deliver steel in the area. He said he believed the tape that had been sent by Wearside Jack to police was an "indirect act of God" which served as a diversion. Sutcliffe told the jury: "I thought it was a diversion so I could be left to carry on. It served to take a great deal of the investigation elsewhere." He said he had nothing to do with the sending of the tape.

A former friend of the Ripper, Trevor Birdsall, of Bradford, giving evidence at the Old Bailey, was asked by Sir Michael Havers, the Attorney General, if he remembered hearing a tape recording by the hoaxer which became known as the Ripper tape. "Yes, I think I heard it," said Mr Birdsall. "I thought there was no chance at all it could be him. It destroyed the link."

Sir Michael told the court: "The harsh truth is that the author of the letters and tape has nothing to do with this case. That person's wicked behaviour may be responsible for casting a shadow over the lives of many innocent people. For my part I cannot condemn too strongly this cruel hoax."

The judge in the trial, Mr Justice Boreham, said: "The scent was falsified by a cynical, almost inhuman, hoaxer - I refer to the tape and letters. I express the hope that one day he may be exposed."

The mother of Jacqueline Hill, Doreen, who still lives near Middlesbrough, told reporters her daughter would probably still be alive if the police had not been distracted by the tape. "The hoaxer has a few murders on his conscience," said Mrs Hill.

Mrs Hill was probably right. Peter Sutcliffe, who was questioned and eliminated from inquiries several times because he did not have a Wearside accent, killed three women between the broadcasting of the hoax tape in June, 1979, and his arrest. The victims were student Barbara Leach, 20, in September, 1979, Marguerite Walls, aged 47, who was found dead in August, 1980, in Farsley, West Yorkshire, and his last victim, Jacqueline Hill.

If the third and final letter from Wearside Jack, which was posted in Sunderland to police and postmarked March 23, 1979, is also considered, it is possible that the killing of 19-year-old student Josephine Whitaker in Halifax in April, 1979, could also have been avoided. For it was the contents of that letter which convinced George Oldfield that the man they were hunting was from Sunderland.

After the Ripper trial, the calls for police to catch the hoaxer were loud and strong, particularly in Sunderland where thousands of men had been living under a cloud of suspicion. If for the 18 months between the broadcasting of the tape and the arrest of Sutcliffe they had been fingered as a serial killer, that accusation, at least, could not now be levelled. But what could was the suspicion that they had sent the callous hoax letters and tape.

The day after Sutcliffe's arrest, voice expert Stanley Ellis, from the University of Leeds, finally admitted the inevitable. He told the Sunderland Echo that he believed the tape and letters were a hoax. But he added: "I remain firmly convinced that the man who made the tape did come from Castletown." He said he believed police may have have interviewed the hoaxer but had ruled him out for other reasons.

After the trial of Sutcliffe, the Sunderland Echo's Assistant Editor Deric Walker, who had travelled to Wakefield, West Yorkshire, to hear the tape almost two years earlier at a Press conference, wrote a strongly-worded editorial. He said: "The hoaxer must still be found, not least because he may still be a killer. Even if he is not, he has been responsible for the most massive waste of police time and money in criminal history."

A Press Association report of the same day said: "Detectives now believe the letters and tape message in which a chilling voice proclaimed 'I'm Jack', were nothing more than an amazing hoax. There may even have been an attempt by one killer to shift the blame for his crime on to the real Ripper."

On May 23, 1981, after Sutcliffe started a life sentence for his crimes, the headline on the front page of the Sunderland Echo read: "Get The Hoaxer". By December, 1981, it appeared the hunt for Wearside Jack had been scaled down. The headline in the Sunderland Echo of December 29 read: "Ripper: Hunt for Hoaxer Cools Off".

Had every effort been made to find Wearside Jack or were police in Sunderland and West Yorkshire just happy to have caught Sutcliffe, the serial killer? Ripper Squad officers have given mixed views in their answers to that question during research for this book. On balance, it would appear the police effort to catch Wearside Jack was weak.

West Yorkshire police were delighted to have caught Britain's most wanted man, even if the arrest of Sutcliffe was nothing more than a fluke. And their colleagues in Sunderland, who had worked so hard with them, were equally delighted the serial killer was behind bars.

Euphoria swept through police stations in West Yorkshire and Wearside on the day of Sutcliffe's arrest. Police officers punched the air, as if the battle was over and they had won; the motor patrol officers in Sheffield who arrested the Ripper were congratulated more than once. Indeed, for all the Ripper Squad officers, management delivered a huge collective pat on the back. And in Sunderland's Gill Bridge Police Station there was a party; a bit of a wild party, by all accounts.

But what about the hunt for Wearside Jack?

Detective Constable Tommy Jackson, of West Yorkshire Police, says: "After the Ripper was arrested, the inquiry was still ongoing to find the hoaxer. There was a team kept on in Sunderland and one in West Yorkshire. The hoaxer wasn't completely forgotten."

But other Ripper Squad officers disagree. One says: "I remember there was a big party down at Gill Bridge when the Ripper was caught. The club was packed out and everyone was celebrating. We had spent all that time looking for the Ripper and he had finally been caught. At that time no one was bothered about the hoaxer. We were just relieved that it was all over.

"As far as we were concerned, our inquiry was over the day the Ripper was arrested. When the Ripper was caught I was fairly certain the hoaxer would be caught within 12 months. But, to be honest, no one was interested.

"Although he had wasted money and police resources, he hadn't caused anyone violence in this area and they had the man that had in West Yorkshire. Whoever the hoaxer was, he has done bloody well to keep it quiet all these years. He could be dead now."

Another Ripper Squad officer, who also does not wish to be named, says: "After the arrest, I don't think everything that could have been done to catch the hoaxer was done. The whole inquiry had been scaled down.

"At the end of the day, it was West Yorkshire police who believed the Ripper was a Sunderland man and had put so much focus on the Sunderland area. It was West Yorkshire's inquiry. Efforts probably were made to catch the hoaxer, but I can't remember anything specific from the inquiry after the Ripper's arrest."

One thing the officer, a former detective, can remember from the inquiry, which was never made public, was the possibility that there was a second tape made by Wearside Jack, his voice having been recorded by the Tyne and Wear Fire Brigade at its headquarters in Pilgrim Street, Newcastle.

He says: "There was a set of strange coincidences in Castletown just after Sutcliffe was arrested. Within about three months a call was received by the fire brigade in Newcastle from a 'phone box in Castletown which turned out to be a hoax.

"The girl who took the call had heard the tape and she was positive that the voice she was hearing was the same man on the tape. She was so convinced that she told her senior officer, and he told her to keep the line open while they traced the call.

Detective Constable George Virtue plays the "I'm Jack" tape to two elderly men in the north of Sunderland. But was there a second recording of Jack's voice, made by the Tyne and Wear Fire Brigade? One Ripper Squad officer says there was. Picture: *The Daily Mail.*

"Three weeks later, the same man made another hoax call to the fire brigade, but this time he dialled 999. In the previous call he had just 'phoned the brigade's main number in Newcastle. The second call was recorded and it was traced to the same 'phone box from where the first call was made.

"The tape of the man's voice was given to the voice expert, who compared it to the Ripper tape, and he said he was at least 80 per cent sure it was the same man. That made Davey Zackrisson's antennae go and it was decided to keep observations on the 'phone box to try to catch the hoaxer. All the men who used the 'phone box were housed - what I mean by that is police followed them to their homes to check out their details.

"That inquiry went on for several weeks, if not months, but the hoax calls to the fire brigade had stopped. There was no more from that 'phone box. But once police had started knocking on doors again that's not surprising, because in Castletown word had spread like wildfire, and that line of inquiry went dead."

Other Ripper Squad officers who were asked about the second "Wearside Jack" tape said they had no knowledge of it. But they add that, after the arrest of the Ripper, their part in the inquiry had come to an end. One says: "I had never heard anything about that story, but then again I moved to another division after the arrest of the Ripper."

Inquiries to the Tyne and Wear Fire Brigade on the existence of a second tape have drawn a blank. Requests for interviews with former Detective Inspector Dave Zackrisson, and the voice expert Stanley Ellis, have also been turned down.

If a second tape did exist there was never any publicity, locally, regionally, or nationally. So the story of the second tape can only remain a claim by a former Ripper Squad officer.

But police in the Ripper inquiry were always very keen to control the information that was given out to the public via the newspapers, radio, and television. A detective sergeant in the West Yorkshire Ripper Squad ended up in court and was fined for giving out information on the inquiry without the authorisation of his senior officers.

West Yorkshire Police spent £1million on publicising the hoax tape and letters. But there were certain things the public could not be told, as that might have jeopardised the whole hunt for the Ripper/Wearside Jack.

We know now that one of the extracts from one of the hoax letters referred to Vera Millward, a Ripper victim, and the hospital she attended for treatment. When police in Sunderland took samples of suspects' handwriting they asked them to write down a certain phrase, "How's your Elsie doing in hospital", is believed to have been the wording. Suspects were asked to write in their normal handwriting and to print the passages they were dictated.

Other information never made public before this book was published include certain evidential links between the forensic evidence at the scene of the Ripper killings and the killer. Police also never revealed that they examined sketches on beer mats, drawn by John Gaffney, during their inquiry.

And there's more.

There was information in the first letter from Wearside Jack to West Yorkshire's Assistant Chief Constable George Oldfield which first gave police the possible Sunderland link in the Ripper inquiry.

That information, never before made public, not only points to the possibility that Wearside Jack is a cruel hoaxer, but also, possibly, a murderer. And it also gives us something that has remained a mystery for 20 years - Wearside Jack's real motive for the hoax of the century.

That information can now be made public.

CHAPTER FOURTEEN

The Unsolved Murder

Mother-of-two Joan Mary Harrison, 26, lived in East View, Deepdale, Preston, Lancashire, with her landlord David Keighley, aged 47. She began renting a room from Mr Keighley in about July, 1975, and paid rent of £4.50 a week.

Mrs Harrison, originally from Chorley, Lancashire, had been separated from her estranged husband Paul Raymond Harrison, 27, a carpet fitter, for about two years. One of her two daughters lived at home with her mother in Chorley and her second daughter had been taken into care by Preston social services.

Mrs Harrison began a relationship with Mr Keighley and, according to a report in Preston's main evening newspaper, the Lancashire Evening Post, they intended to marry. Mr Keighley told the Post:: "We were very close. We were engaged to be married and I had bought her a ring.

"She had her problems but I tried to show her the better side of life, staying at home at night, sitting by the fire and watching television instead of fooling around the town.

"I told her I didn't care what she had done in the past - it was now that counted. I fell in love with her and I couldn't wait to get back home at night to see her. She got under my skin. She looked after me. She used to cook and clean up and one of the last things she did was to trim the Christmas tree.

"I'm no drinker but she did use to have too much. She sometimes came back tipsy but she was a good tenant and I can't say a bad word against her."

It was her heavy drinking and use of drugs that led to the breakdown of her second marriage, her husband, Paul Harrison, told the coroner at the inquest into her death. Mrs Harrison, who was unemployed and claiming social security but had worked as a machinist and shop assistant, was also an asthmatic.

On a Thursday evening, Mrs Harrison left her home in the Avenham area of Preston for a night out. She was dressed in clothes which were fashionable in the mid 1970s. She was wearing a turqoise/blue jumper with a bright yellow tank top over it, dark brown trousers, and brown, suede, calf-length boots.

It wasn't a warm night and Mrs Harrison had on a light green, three-quarter-length coat with an imitation fur collar. The coat, which was reasonably smart, would keep out the biting November winds as she walked along the town centre streets in Preston.

Mrs Harrison did not have a lot of jewellery, but she kept some of it in her small, black, shiny handbag, which had two silver fasteners on the side. Inside her handbag were two gold wedding rings, an engagement ring with three stones set in platinum, several silver or chrome bracelets and a yellow metal, novelty key ring which contained the words "hands off" or "keep off".

She also had a man's wristwatch and two cigarette lighters. One was a Varaflame lighter, the other, made in Japan, was a Triumph Crystal lighter. It was believed Mrs Harrison's handbag may have also contained a diary, though she did not make many detailed entries, and an inhaler, used by asthmatics.

After she left home to go to a local nightclub, Mrs Harrison was not seen for two days and three nights.

On a Sunday morning, Ronald Atkinson, 47, of Guildford Road, Preston, left his home to go to work. Minutes later, his wife, Mildred, also 47, took her usual morning stroll to the newsagents to collect the Sunday newspapers.

In Berwick Road, at the rear of Frenchwood Street, where Joan Harrison used to lodge, a slightly open door on a derelict lock-up garage was banging and flapping in the wind. Mrs Atkinson, a mother-of-five, caught a glimpse of what she thought, at first, was the body of a drunken man.

She told the Lancashire Evening Post: "The door was blowing open and I saw the body lying face down. There was a coat over her head and I saw blood on the ground beside her. I did not know it was a woman. I thought it might be a drunk who had banged his head."

What she had seen was the body of Joan Harrison, who had been battered to death in what Detective Superintendent Wilf Brooks, second-in-command at Lancashire CID, told the Post was a "savage attack" with no obvious motive.

Three hours later, after detectives and forensic experts had completed their inquiries at the murder scene, Mrs Harrison's body was taken away in a hearse. The dead woman's handbag, containing the jewellery and other personal items, including a brown leather purse, was missing from the murder scene.

After the post-mortem examination, carried out at Preston Royal Infirmary by pathologist Dr John Benstead, police were still not able to determine the exact cause of death, nor pinpoint the time. Det Supt Brooks said he could not confirm or deny there had been a sexual motive to the killing.

Eighty detectives from Preston county police headquarters and the regional crime squad were involved in the murder hunt. Police dogs were drafted in to scour the banks of the River Ribble and the open spaces of Avenham Park in the search for the victim's missing handbag.

Detectives also carried out inquiries in Preston's pubs and clubs. Police said Mrs Harrison was a regular visitor to town centre pubs

Det Supt Brooks said: "I am anxious to know from anyone who knows of anybody who went missing suddenly from Preston since Thursday at 10.25pm up until Sunday at 8am.

Neighbours were interviewed as police began house-to-house inquiries. According to neighbours, No 3 Frenchwood Street, which had the derelict lock-up garage at the rear where Mrs Harrison's battered body was found, had been sold to the council and had been empty for a month.

A council spokesman said the house was due to be inspected and re-let.

While murder squad detectives were carrying out their inquiries, reporters on the Lancashire Evening Post were making inquiries of their own into Mrs Harrison's lifestyle. Those inquiries led to a front page story in the Post on Tuesday, November 25, 1975, headlined: "Twilight world of a murder victim"

The story, which did not carry the author's byline, read: "Detectives are probing Preston's twilight world in their hunt for the killer of 26-year-old mother-of-two Mrs Joan Harrison.

"They are sifting through the lives of tramps, winos, and down-and-outs in their investigation into the seamy side of Preston.

"Inquiries have revealed that Mrs Harrison was part of Preston's 'Skid Row'. She wasn't averse to drinking cider from the bottle in back-street derelict property. Detectives ... have been hampered by the blurred memories of some of her friends ... the town centre drinkers.

"Just off Preston's town centre Church Street, the Post talked to three men who were about to start a can or two of cider. They knew Mrs Harrison. What they knew is not all pleasant.

"One said: 'Aye, we knew her all right. It was Wednesday when I saw her last. She used to come down here quite a lot for a drink and the rest'."

Det Supt Brooks said: "Our inquiries have been more protracted by the lifestyle of some of the woman's friends."

Further police inquiries revealed that on the day she disappeared, Mrs Harrison had been at the St Mary's Hostel for Homeless Men in Preston where she had a voluntary job as a part-time cleaner. The hostel's warden, Ian Pinchen, reported her missing on Saturday morning - the day before she was found dead.

He said: "Joan was a kind sort of girl, good natured as a rule. She knew quite a lot of the residents. She had seen the rougher side of life. But Joan used to drink too much for her own good. That was the cause of many of her problems."

Later the same week, police revealed that Mrs Harrison had had sex shortly before she was killed.

Det Supt Brooks said: "I am now satisfied that there were very strong sexual implications and aspects to this murder. The woman had had sex shortly before she died."

By the end of the first week of the murder inquiry, police had interviewed 3,000 people and had taken 1,000 statements.

Det Supt Brooks said inquiries were being widened to take into account lorry drivers who were known to park in Preston town centre and visit pubs there on a Friday night. There had been a report that Mrs Harrison was last sighted on the Friday morning after she went missing.

Following the forensic evidence that indicated Mrs Harrison had had sex before she was killed, police began taking saliva samples from residents living in the Avenham area of the town.

Det Supt Brooks said: "We are requesting the full co-operation of the public in carrying out these tests, which will be taken for forensic examination." Certain people interviewed by police had already given samples.

At that time, when police were not aware there was a serial killer on the loose battering women to death with a hammer, murder squad detectives believed the killing of Mrs Harrison was not linked to any other murders or violent attacks in the Lancashire area or further afield.

But, as in all major inquiries, checks were made with neighbouring forces to see if there were any unsolved murders or violent attacks with which parallels could be drawn in the case of Joan Mary Harrison.

The fact that police were wanting to interview lorry drivers who may have been in Preston on the night of Mrs Harrison's murder was nothing more than coincidental to the later inquiry to find the Yorkshire Ripper/Wearside Jack.

But the murder of Joan Harrison was eventually included as one in the Ripper series. Why?

One Ripper Squad detective says: "The scene of her murder, and the way the body was situated, was just like a Ripper murder scene. There were also very few clues to go on, apart from the forensic evidence, which was another trademark of the Ripper. He left very few clues behind."

Another clue pointing to the murderer of Joan Harrison came to light in March, 1978, when Wearside Jack sent two letters to West Yorkshire's George Oldfield.

In one of the first two letters, believed to be the first he posted in Sunderland on March 8, 1978, Jack said something which made detectives believe the murder of Joan Harrison was a Ripper killing. The words, never before made public, were along the lines of: "How many is it now George? Four or five? What about Preston in 1975? I think you'll find it's six."

Detectives never made known the fact that they received two letters in March, 1978, until they had received the third letter, in March, 1979, and the tape in June, 1979. The reason for that was probably because doubts were cast on the authenticity of the first two letters because the author had failed to mention the murder of Yvonne Pearson, who was murdered before one of the letters was posted, but whose body was found after the letter was received. (This was discussed in an earlier chapter).

But there was a stronger evidential link between the sender of the tape and letters and the killer of Joan Harrison - the forensic evidence at the scene of her killing, the derelict lock-up garage in Preston.

Mrs Harrison had had sex before she was killed. But there were also reports that a part-eaten apple was found at the scene of the crime. Forensic scientists were able to establish the killer had two characteristics: He was of the B secretor blood group and he had an eighth-of-an-inch gap in his top two front teeth.

Forensic scientists can establish if a person is a B secretor by examining bodily fluids such as semen or saliva. B secretors secrete blood antibodies in other bodily fluids, such as saliva or semen. It is estimated that only seven per cent of the population is of the B secretor blood group.

The killer of Joan Harrison had, for some reason, also bit her left breast. Were forensic scientists able to determine the killer's blood group and the gap in his top two front teeth because of saliva in or on her body and the bite on the breast? Or was the saliva and bite mark from the reported part-eaten apple at the scene?

Whichever the source of the clues, they did not point to Peter William Sutcliffe. Although he is of the B blood group, he is not a B secretor. He does not like apples. And he has always maintained that he never had sex with his victims. He told his North East penfriend Olive Curry when she visited him in Broadmoor: "I did not kill that girl".

Peter Sutcliffe admitted killing 13 women and attempting to murder seven more. He was destined to serve life behind bars. What had he to loose by co-operating with police and admitting he killed Joan Harrison? The reason he never admitted her killing can only be that he did not kill her. So who did murder Joan Harrison, and why?

The finger of suspicion can point to Wearside Jack.

The forensic examination of saliva on the letters and tape that Jack sent to police confirmed he was a B secretor. There was also the claim in his first letter that police had failed to take into account one of the "Ripper" killings, that of Joan Harrison in Preston in November, 1975.

In the third letter - which finally sent police on the biggest wild goose chase in British criminal history - Wearside Jack said he had been given information about a hospital one of the Ripper victims, Vera Millward, attended for treatment.

He may have known Vera Millward, but Wearside Jack did not kill her. She was one of the real Ripper victims. He did know Joan Harrison and sending the letters and tape give us his only probable motive - that if he did kill Joan Harrison his elaborate and costly hoax was an attempt to shift blame for the murder onto Peter William Sutcliffe.

But slippery Jack had slipped up. Peter Sutcliffe was having none of it. The murder of Joan Harrison and the hoax of the century are still two unsolved crimes.

What else suggests that Wearside Jack is not only a callous hoaxer, but, possibly, a murderer?

One Ripper Squad detective says one answer could be time, depending on which charge could be brought against Jack, if he's ever caught. The officer says: "At the time he could have been charged with wasting police time, but he couldn't be charged with that offence now.

"The reason for that is there is a time limit for bringing certain prosecutions. As far as I remember wasting police time has a time limit of six months. All this happened about 20 years ago.

"They could try to bring a charge against him of attempting to pervert the course of justice. But, personally, I don't think there's enough to go on to make the charge stick."

Leading Sunderland solicitor Cecil Emmerson disagrees. He says if Jack is ever caught the Crown Prosecution Service would want to bring a charge of attempting to pervert the course of justice, which is an indictable offence at common law, which would be dealt with at crown court.

Mr Emmerson, who has been involved in some of Wearside's most infamous and high-profile criminal cases, including that of Sunderland Strangler Steven Grieveson, acted for a number of people in Sunderland questioned in connection with the Wearside Jack/Yorkshire Ripper inquiry.

Mr Emmerson says: "What the sender of the letters and the tape was saying was, 'I'm the Ripper', and, 'Catch me if you can'. He was attempting to put police and the courts on a false trail. He was attempting to pervert the course of justice or obstructing police. It is 20 years since I gave this any consideration.

Leading Wearside solicitor Cecil Emmerson, who acted for several people questioned in connection with the Ripper/Wearside Jack inquiry. Picture: *The Sunderland Echo.*

"He was giving information which was false which misled police in their investigations. Attempting to pervert the course of justice is an offence at common law. If he ever is caught the courts would not waste their time by prosecuting him on a lesser offence which could be dealt with by magistrates."

Mr Emmerson says as there was such a public outcry at the time of the Ripper inquiry and a suggestion that the hoax cost the lives of at least three women, Jack, if he is still alive and ever caught, could end up spending a lot of years behind bars.

If Jack is also the murderer of Joan Harrison and was convicted of her murder, he would be destined to spend the rest of his life in jail.

Mr Emmerson adds: "I represented a large number of people who had in fact been interviewed concerning this. The object was to get a sample of their voice for analysis. For the most part, once they realised just how many hundreds of people were being interviewed, they treated the matter lightheartedly.

"I can't remember the names of those suggested as likely candidates but I remember the police were very enthusiastic about it all. I think they regarded the letters and tape as something of an irritation because the sender appeared to be cocking a snook at them. I think the police would still be enthusiastic today about finding him."

Is Wearside Jack still alive? What has he been doing all these years? Who is he? Will he ever be caught?

CHAPTER FIFTEEN

A New Suspect?

The "suspects" interviewed by police, who agreed to be interviewed during research for this book, all had interesting and sometimes familiar stories to tell about their recollections of the Ripper/Wearside Jack inquiry. The number of people who came forward to tell their stories is an indication of the impact the inquiry had on their lives and the lives of so many people on Wearside.

In reality there were thousands of "suspects" in the policy inquiry who had to be eliminated. There was little evidence in the hands of police and what they had was circumstantial. But the investigation in Sunderland was extensive and very, very thorough. After 20 years it seems incredible that Wearside Jack was never caught and has yet to be unmasked.

Could it be that Jack had no connection at all with the north of Sunderland and, in particular, with Castletown, the former pit village where linguistics expert Stanley Ellis said he was from? Even after the Ripper was caught Mr Ellis said he still thought Jack was from the Castletown area. But was he? The massive scale of the police investigation would suggest he was not.

The voice on the chilling "I'm Jack" tape was definitely a Wearside voice. The accent was so strong, so immediately identifiable, it had to be a Wearside man. Sunderland is on Wearside but so are the outlying areas of Washington, Houghton-le-Spring, Hetton-le-Hole, Eppleton, Easington Lane, and Fence Houses. Very few of the hundreds of men interviewed were from south Sunderland.

Could it be that Jack was from one of those areas?

If Jack is still alive he will now be aged between 40 and 62. We know he has a distinctive Wearside accent and, if he killed Joan Harrison, a gap in his teeth; that he once possessed a tape recorder and a copy of the song *"Thank you for Being a Friend"* and that he also has a lisp or some other speech impediment. He is also of the B secretor blood group.

From the contents of the hoax letters and tape, *"They never learn, George, do they?"*, it can be assumed that Jack hates women, and his links with prostitutes - he claims to have met Ripper victim Vera Millward - suggest he has difficulty forming relationships, at least sexual relationships. If Jack did kill Joan Harrison in Preston he is also perverted, as Mrs Harrison's murderer bit her breast, either during sex or afterwards.

If Jack did not kill Joan Harrison he is still a hoaxer. Was he a natural practical joker who liked to "wind people up", as they say in Sunderland. And did his Ripper hoax start out as a practical joke that went too far?

On their own, the clues linked only to the tape and letters provide little information on the possible identity of Jack. But, coupled with the evidence linked to the murder of Joan Harrison a fuller, but still incomplete, picture emerges.

If Jack did kill Mrs Harrison, he must have occasionally travelled from Wearside to West Yorkshire. If he had a similar lifestyle to Mrs Harrison, the heavy drinking "down-and-out" as outlined in the Lancashire Evening Post it is that that may have brought them together. For him, a sexually-frustrated inadequate, their meeting was an opportunity for sex. For Mrs Harrison it resulted in her death.

Is it possible that Mrs Harrison met Wearside Jack in St Mary's Hostel for the Homeless in Preston, where she worked as a cleaner?

After her murder in Preston, her known associates were asked to provide a sample of their saliva. And this they did. But Det Supt Wilf Brooks, of Lancashire CID, was still keen to hear from anyone who may have left Preston, for whatever reason, after the killing. Had Jack fled back home to Wearside?

In the later Ripper inquiry, thousands of people on Wearside were asked to provide samples of their saliva. Everyone asked provided a sample and they were analysed by forensic scientists. Scientists were trying to track down the hoaxer who sent the letters. Saliva on the envelopes proved he was a B secretor - the same rare blood type as the killer of Joan Harrison.

Is it possible that Wearside Jack never gave a sample of his saliva to police in Preston in 1975 or to police on Wearside between 1979 and 1981? Is it also possible that, as he had no connection with the north of Sunderland, he was never interviewed?

During my research for this book, sources suggested four names for Wearside Jack. Three, including the name of a retired police officer, were based on the informant's belief that the man they had fingered spoke just like the man on the hoax tape. That was little to go on.

But there was one name that warranted further investigation. During several months of spare-time research, I initially learned nothing about this man that could eliminate him from my own inquiries. Indeed, as the research progressed, evidence against him, albeit circumstantial, continued to mount.

The potential "new suspect", whom I'll call Jack, was made known to me by a source, whom I'll call Terry. Terry has not been paid for providing me with this information and he did not go to the police with it 20 years ago because he considered Jack a friend. To some extent he still does, thus the reason he wishes to remain anonymous.

Terry says: "It has been on my conscience for 20 years and every time I read or hear a story about the Yorkshire Ripper I think about (Jack) and wonder whether or not I should have gone to the police at the time. I need to know for sure whether or not he was the hoaxer."

This is what Terry has to say about Jack:

'He had deep-set eyes and cheekbones, as if he had never had any sleep. He was just a drop-out and he had no timing in life. He woke up, he went out and just walked from here to there.

He had no family, other than his father, but his father has since died.

He would sleep anywhere. I remember once he slept in a haystack because on a Sunday afternoon when we were in the pub he came in and you could see he had been sleeping in the hay. There were pieces of straw in his hair.

I knew him for a few years, off and on. I would never see him for weeks and then he would just turn up, out of the blue.

I first met him in a workingmen's club. He just came up to me and asked me if I wanted a pint. He would always ask if you wanted a pint, if he had the money. He was always alone.

One night he wanted me to hear something. He started dictating one of the hoax letters and it was word perfect. I wasn't really interested and didn't think much about it until later. He had read the letter out loud word for word.

The way (Jack) was reading it out you would think he had rehearsed it. How could he have known the full thing?

To me it appeared he was looking for help. He wanted help. He was wanting me to run around and tell him I was going to 'phone the police.

When he said the letter, I wasn't looking at him. And he's on with this thing, saying it and saying it. Certain words were clicking. It was like someone reading a story and that's how it stuck in my mind.

It was unbelievable the way he read it off. He never got a word wrong. He wasn't the type of person that could do that, unless he wrote it all down and rehearsed it.

I was convinced it was him because he trusted in me. He asked me, 'Do you think that was like the Ripper?' He wanted me to tell him it did sound exactly like the Ripper. It's funny, but after that he seemed to go all to pot.

When we used to talk about the Ripper he would always say he has got them on a wild goose chase.

He wanted it off his shoulders because it had escalated too much. He's the type of man that if you put him in jail, he wouldn't be worried. It's just like bed and breakfast to him. He would often say things like, 'Nobody can say it like me'. (Referring to the tape).

When the Ripper thing was happening he used to steal women's underwear. It was funny that at the same time the Ripper thing was going on he was doing this. He used to say black underwear was the best.

He was a joker but he got on people's nerves, but he never really hurt anyone. I liked him as a person. He was a laugh.

He got the nickname (Jack) the Ripper because of the way he used to talk about women. He called women more than he called men. A lot of people thought he hated women.

When there was a group of women talking or laughing he would think they were talking about him or laughing at him

He never had a girlfriend and he never married. He would have liked someone to have taken him on. But it was his ways, and that, that put women off.

He had been in trouble with the police. He knew different police officers by name. He must have been caught shoplifting. He went shoplifting once and got chucked out of the shop. He would steal things just to get a pint, not to make money.

One night he said to me, 'I'm going down to Doncaster. If there's any work you want, I'll get it for you'. He used to say he knew Doncaster like the back of his hand. He used to just jump on a train and go somewhere and he wouldn't be back for a few days.

He was the kind of character who wanted to be recognised. He was the type of person you would think you would only see in a film. You would think there couldn't be anyone one like that in real life. He was over the moon when he walked into a club and somebody said, 'There's (Jack)'.

He was never violent to anyone. He would only speak violently. He was fit and never seemed to ail anything. I made a copy of a music tape for him once, so he must have had a tape recorder. I don't know if he has a gap in his teeth, but he does have a lisp. '

Terry's suspicion that his friend was Wearside Jack was based on what he had come to know about the man over several years. His voice, to Terry, sounded just like the man on the tape. And when Jack was able to recite one of the letters word perfect, it made Terry even more suspicious.

But Terry was not aware, and during this research was not made aware, of the other facts, or circumstantial evidence, that suggested he could possibly be right.

From information provided by Terry, Ripper Squad officers, other "suspects" and from other sources, the circumstantial evidence included:

- The sender of the hoax tape had a lisp - Jack has a lisp.
- The only reason Terry gave me the information was because it "has been on my conscience for 20 years". He did not ask for any money.
- The killer of Joan Harrison hated women, *"They never learn, do they George"* - Jack hated women and was always sounding off about them.
- The killer of Joan Harrison was from Wearside and sometimes travelled to West Yorkshire - Jack travelled regularly and can be placed in West Yorkshire (though not, at this stage, in Preston in 1975).
- The murder of Joan Harrison was sexually motivated (she had had sex before she died and the bite on the breast etc): Jack was a pervert, who stole women's underwear from clothes lines during the Ripper inquiry. He has never married and never been seen with a girlfriend.
- In 1979 the hoaxer had a portable tape recorder - Jack had a portable tape recorder that year.
- The hoaxer had an LP from which he taped the song "*Thank you for Being a Friend*" by Andrew Gold : Jack, a petty thief, used to steal LPs from local shops at the time.

- The hoax letters and tape were posted in Sunderland by someone who travelled to West Yorkshire - Jack would be away from Sunderland for varying periods.

- Jack could recite the entire contents of one of the hoax letters without error and sounded exactly the same.

From what Terry told me, and the information I had been able to obtain from my research, there was very little evidence to suggest Terry's friend (Jack), could be a new suspect.

But there was also, unknown to Terry, possible links between his friend and the murder of Joan Harrison. She was a "down and out" and a heavy drinker. Jack was a "down and out" and a heavy drinker. Jack also travelled regulary. Was he in Preston in November, 1975, and did he stay at St Mary's Hostel where Joan Harrison worked?

A Ripper Squad officer says that as Jack had used the word "uniform" (a job word) rather than "uniformed" in the hoax letters, it was suspected he was a police officer. Could it be that Jack, a petty thief, used the "job" word because of his many run-ins with police?

The information that Terry was able to give me spurred me into finding out more about Jack. I knew where he lived. But I could not confront him directly - that could blow the whole thing.

On a night in March, 1999, Terry arranged to meet Jack in a Wearside pub. I agreed to join the pair later the same evening. I was soon to discover whether Jack was a "new suspect".

The evidence I had on Jack was purely circumstantial. The fact that he fitted the hoaxer's "offender profile" in some ways could have applied to many other people. I needed more evidence. It was possible, probable even, that Jack had nothing to do with the hoax or the murder.

There were three things I needed from Jack: A sample of his handwriting to compare with that in the hoax letters; a recording of his voice to compare with that on the hoax tape; and, if possible, a sample of his saliva to forward on to a forensic scientist who could determine whether or not Jack was of the rare B secretor blood group.

Terry and I had been in contact by telephone three times during the day. When the night arrived, I equipped myself with a small tape recorder, a pen, two or three pieces of paper, and an envelope. Could Jack really be Wearside Jack?

As I walked towards the pub I switched the tape recorder on to the "voice activated" switch and a little red light could be seen deep down in my outside front jacket pocket. It was not something Jack would notice, I thought, as I entered the small bar of the old-fashioned, spit-and-sawdust type pub.

In the pub, a tough-looking barman was wiping the counter with a beer cloth, three men stood at the bar near the corner of the room drinking and talking and three others were sitting at an untidy table on which stood an ash tray overflowing with cigarette ends. One of the men was Terry and one of the other two - I knew not which - was Jack.

I said hello to Terry, bought a half of lager at the bar, and sat at their table. Terry's two acquaintances eyed me with suspicion but then one, who was drunk, singing loudly one minute and laughing loudly the next, put his hand out to shake mine. "I've had 18 bottles of brown ale today," said the man, as I shook his hand.

"Who are you?", I asked. The drunken man replied: "I'm the boy! That's me. I'm the boy!"

"The boy" was a foul-mouthed, aggressive, drunken, down-and-out. He appeared to be aged in his 50s. He had a strong Wearside accent, but his voice did not sound like Jack's. I looked at his mouth. He did not have a gap in his teeth.

I glanced at Terry who tilted his head towards the man on his left. The message was non verbal but clear. I had been looking at the wrong man.

Jack was in his fifties, and he looked his age. His hair was grey, collar-length, and appeared to be dirty, but he was not receding. He had high cheek bones and a protruding chin, with a day or two's-worth of stubble. His features were angular and, facially, he slightly resembled the aging film star Jack Palance.

He was wearing a second hand suit and a shirt and tie. His clothes were dirty and creased, but not filthy. They were the type that could be found in any of the many charity shops in Sunderland and Houghton.

In the dim light of the bar I could see no gap in his teeth. I moved closer. His teeth were false.

Then, above the drunken ramblings of the "the boy" sitting opposite, I listened to his voice. It was a strong Wearside voice; a Sunderland dialect. Jack was unmistakably a "mackem". He spoke slowly and deliberately, starting and ending a sentence without an "uhm", "err"or other pause in between. There was also something else easily detectable. He had a lisp.

He was exactly as Terry had outlined.

Certain words and phrases he used, and the rythym of his speech, as well as his lisp and his accent, made me believe his voice did sound similar to the voice on the hoax tape. It couldn't sound exactly the same; Jack and his voice had aged 20 years. I had his voice on tape but I still needed a sample of his handwriting and a sample of his saliva.

After two more pints Jack was comfortable in my company and I appeared to have gained his confidence. It was now time to put another plan into action to extract handwriting from Jack and a sample of his saliva.

I did that by persuading Jack to write his address on an envelope and for him to seal it down. However, he printed the address (only one of the hoax envelopes had a printed address). I later discovered the recording I had of his voice was poor because of background noise.

Terry and I arranged a second meeting with Jack in the same pub. This time I needed a sample of his ordinary writing, in lower case or "longhand" and a better recording of his voice. I also hoped to find out more about Jack's personal history.

Jack had been living in a bed and breakfast hostel on Wearside for at least part of 1998. The hostel was known locally as a "Doss House", as all the residents had their rent and meals paid for by the Department of Social Security.

It was home to some alcoholics, former care in the community patients who had mental health problems, to some people who had just ended jail terms and to refugees who had fled war torn former Yugoslavia.

It was an environment that Jack, a down-and-out traveller who could sleep anywhere, would have found familiar.

At our second meeting there were some things I learned about Jack that suggested he could not be a "new suspect". One was the fact that he had once been interviewed by Ripper Squad police.

But there was one thing that Jack told me voluntarily that was of some significance. He told me he had lived in Preston for a year in a "bedsit" 24 years earlier. That placed Jack in the same town as Joan Harrison at the time she was murdered. Did Jack, a down-and-out drinker, ever meet Joan Harrison? By the time I put that question to Jack, he was too drunk to answer and too drunk to care.

I managed to obtain a sample of Jack's normal longhand handwriting and took that, along with the envelope from our first meeting on which he printed his address, to handwriting expert Diane Simpson the next day in Chester. Mrs Simpson was THE expert on Wearside Jack's handwriting, as she was called in by George Oldfield 20 years earlier to analyse the writing on the hoax letters. Mrs Simpson analysed the new material and was able to give an answer almost immediately.

CHAPTER SIXTEEN

The Handwriting

At the height of the hunt for the Ripper/Wearside Jack, West Yorkshire Police produced a four-page newspaper about the "largest manhunt ever undertaken". Thousands of copies were published and circulated nationally but, as ever, the main areas of distribution were West Yorkshire and Wearside.

The headline on the front page was a simple plea "Help Us Catch the Ripper" and a paragraph at the top of the page, in bold type, set the scene. It read: "For the past four years a vicious killer has been at large in the North of England. There have been to date 12 horrific murders and four brutal attacks. The evidence suggests that the same man may be responsible for all of them. If so, he has struck 13 times in West Yorkshire, twice in Manchester and once in Lancashire. Large teams of police officers, including Regional Crime Squads, are working full time in West Yorkshire, Sunderland, Manchester and Lancashire to catch him. His original targets were prostitutes but innocent girls have also died. You can help end this terror ..."

In the centre pages of the publication there were more details of the man police were seeking and 12 single columns of copy were given over to the known Ripper victims. Each of the columns carried a picture of the murdered woman. Victims Marguerite Walls, killed in Farsley, West Yorkshire in August, 1980, and student Jacqueline Hill, killed in Leeds in November, 1980, were not featured. Their killings had yet to take place. And there was one of the killings featured in the centre pages, that of Joan Harrison in Preston in 1975, which should not have been there. Mrs Harrison, it was discovered later, was probably not one of the Ripper victims.

The newspaper also carried details of "four vicious assaults" by the Ripper on women who had escaped his clutches. They were Anna Rogulskyj, a 34-year-old from Keighley, who was attacked in July, 1975; Olive Smelt, attacked by the Ripper in August, 1975; Maureen Long, attacked in Bradford in July, 1977, and Marilyn Moore who was left for dead with a fractured skull after she was attacked in Leeds in December, 1977.

Maureen Long was known to one of the thousands of "suspects" in Sunderland interviewed by Ripper Squad police on the trail of Wearside Jack. Ron Fulbirg (mentioned in an earlier chapter), who lives in north Sunderland, was arrested and questioned 14 times about the killings and the hoax tape and letters. In early 1999 he said he had yet to be eliminated from the hoaxer inquiry and the inquiry into the murder of Joan Harrison. He denied any involvement in the killing or the hoax.

It was the hoax letters and tape that resulted in a lot of false information being included in the "Help Us Catch The Ripper" publication. The thousands of people who provided police with information after reading the newspaper had been deceived into believing they knew a potential suspect. They had been deceived not by police, who geniunely believed they were on the right track, but by Wearside Jack, the hoaxer of the century.

It was his hoax that resulted in readers being asked a series of questions about people they knew who may have fitted the general description of the Yorkshire Ripper. The first question asked was: "Has (he) a Wearside accent?" Readers were also asked to read a sample of the suspect's handwriting, which was reproduced on the back page of the newspaper, and to telephone the "Ripper Hotline" to hear the tape, if they hadn't already done so.

The reward for information leading to the arrest and conviction of the Ripper/Wearside Jack stood at £30,000. The reward fund had started in February, 1978, during the police investigation into the death of Helen Rytka. Yorkshire Post Newspapers had put up £5,000, a further £5,000 was offered by the Northamptonshire Evening Telegraph, the local newspaper in Barbara Leach's home town of Kettering, and £20,000 had been offered from West Yorkshire Police Authority funds.

West Yorkshire Police were keen to stress just how extensive the "largest manhunt ever undertaken" was, even if that meant informing the public about the unconventional or unorthodox "expertise" sought from outside of the police service. "Expertise outside the field of conventional police personnel has also been involved at various stages," said a report in the newspaper. "Consultant psychiatrists were among the first professional bodies to be involved in the early months of the murder series.

"Since then a graphologist has given us the benefit of her insight into the killer through a study of his handwriting; hypnotism has been used on one or two of the killer's surviving victims to obtain even minute details which the conscious mind had forgotten; forensic scentists and pathologists have constantly been involved."

The graphologist, or handwriting expert, called in by Ripper Squad police to analyse the letters sent by Wearside Jack was Diane Simpson, of Diane Simpson Associates, who is based in Chester. Mrs Simpson drew up a long and detailed report after analysing Jack's handwriting and some of the information she provided to police was used in drawing up the offender profile of the Ripper/Wearside Jack.

For the past four years a vicious killer has been at large in the North of England. There have been to date 12 horrific murders and four brutal attacks. The evidence suggests that the same man may be responsible for all of them. If so, he has struck 13 times in West Yorkshire, twice in Manchester and once in Lancashire. Large teams of police officers, including Regional Crime Squads, are working full time in West Yorkshire, Sunderland, Manchester and Lancashire to catch him. His original targets were prostitutes but innocent girls have also died. You can help to end this terror . . .

HELP US CATCH THE RIPPER

● HAVE YOU SEEN THE HANDWRITING?

IF YOU HAVEN'T IT'S ON THE BACK PAGE

● HAVE YOU HEARD THE TAPE?

IF YOU HAVEN'T, RING THE NEAREST OF THE FOLLOWING TELEPHONE NUMBERS:

LEEDS (0532) 464111
MANCHESTER (061) 246 8060
BRADFORD (0274) 36511
NEWCASTLE (0632) 8075

DO ANY OF THESE QUESTIONS DESCRIBE SOMEONE YOU KNOW?

- Has a Wearside (Geordie) accent?
- Is physically fit and reasonably strong?
- Travels between, or has connections in, the Yorkshire, Lancashire and Sunderland areas?
- Perhaps shows disgust of low moral standards?
- Is a manual worker or has access to tools?
- Possibly lives alone or with aged parents?
- Is prone to sudden outbursts of emotion?
- Owns a car of his own or has access to one?
- Sometimes stays out late at night?

- BUT DON'T DISCOUNT ANY SUSPICIONS BECAUSE OF THE QUESTIONS. IF YOU HAVE ANY DOUBTS AT ALL, CONTACT THE POLICE AND HELP CATCH THE RIPPER.

IF YOU ARE AN EMPLOYER

- Does your firm possibly have business connections throughout the North of England, especially in the Yorkshire, Lancashire and Sunderland areas.
- Have you an employee who was available in Sunderland to post an envelope on the following dates:
  March 7/8, 1978.
  March 12/13, 1978.
  March 21/22, 1979.
  Shortly before June 18, 1979.

Through his duties or being absent from work was he available to attack the 'Ripper' victims (see centre pages) on:

July 5, 1975.	February 6, 1977.	December 14, 1977.
August 15, 1975.	April 24, 1977.	January 21, 1978.
October 30, 1975.	June 26, 1977.	January 31, 1978.
November 20, 1975.	July 10, 1977.	May 17, 1978.
January 20, 1976.	October 1, 1977.	April 5, 1979.
		September 2, 1979.

The front page of the newspaper produced by West Yorkshire Police and printed by EXPRESSprint of Wakefield. Thousands of copies were distributed across the country in the hunt for the Ripper/Wearside Jack.

IS THE KILLER WE WANT KNOWN TO YOU?

Is he your next door neighbour? Or a workmate or colleague? Perhaps a relative or friend? The person next to you?

Someone who lives a very ordinary life during the day and probably appears quite normal but intermittently becomes a savage killer once darkness descends?

Twelve horrific murders stand as mute testimony to his double life.

But the fact is that someone knows him, like the rest of us he has relatives and friends and earns his living at some occupation.

He has been described as a 'homicidal maniac' and 'psychopathic killer' which is another way of saying he doesn't care who his next victim is. Bear in mind that although he had attacked many women who were in some way social outcasts, his catalogue of terror also lists respectable women.

He last struck in Bradford on September 2. His victim was pretty 20 year old Bradford University student Barbara Leach taking a late night stroll after an enjoyable Saturday night out.

Don't forget — next time it could be your daughter, wife or girlfriend.

West Yorkshire's Assistant Chief Constable (Crime) Mr. George Oldfield, the man leading the 'Ripper' hunt, believes the tape recording shows the man to have a Wearside (Geordie) accent.

With that in mind his appeal to firms with business connections in the Sunderland and Yorkshire areas becomes all that more urgent.

Mr. Oldfield says, "We believe the man responsible is a manual worker. He could be a lorry driver. He could be engaged in a firm fitting double glazing and travelling about the country. But we do feel he is a working man as opposed to an office type.

"I am asking firms whether any of their employees — skilled, semi-skilled or unskilled were engaged on work in the Sunderland or Tyneside area on any of the following dates — 7th or 8th March 1978, 12th or 13 March 1978, 21st or 22nd March 1979 or shortly before the 18th June 1979.

"I would like firms in the North East, including Tyneside, to let me know whether employees from firms in Yorkshire were engaged on maintenance, repair or installation work on their premises on any of those dates.

"It would be helpful for me to know from employers in Yorkshire who are engaged in the engineering field, in its broadest terms, details of employees who were off work on the dates mentioned".

Over the past four years Mr. Oldfield has learned much about the man he is hunting and has built up a picture of a killer who can strike at any time.

"I believe him to be white, over 20 years old, at least average to above average height and an artisan or manual worker".

Mr. Oldfield adds, "I think he may live or work in West Yorkshire or close to the area and in all probability lives alone, or with aged parent or parents and that he has connections with the Sunderland area".

The CID Chief says he wants firms to check their records and respond to his appeal whether or not they turn up positive results. In that way he hopes not to have to contact firms later only to find that checks have already been done.

Is he your next door neighbour? Or a workmate or colleague? Perhaps a relative or friend? The person next to you? asks the report on Page 2 of the newspaper. Thousands of men came under suspicion in the hunt for the Ripper/Wearside Jack.

PRESTON

JOAN HARRISON

November 20, 1975

At 26 years old Joan Harrison was a sad character. Once she had been a houseproud and loving mother to her two young children.

But following the separation from her husband the children were taken into care and her life took a downward path.

On November 20, 1975, she spent much of the day drinking and then spent several hours at a local hostel for the homeless in Preston, Lancashire. Mrs. Harrison was last seen alive at 10.20 pm in Church Street walking towards Preston town centre.

Her body was found at 8 am on November 23 in a disused garage in Berwick Road.

Lancashire detectives quickly noted the similar circumstances which had surrounded the death of Wilma McCann in Leeds a month earlier and to consider a possible link between the two.

Later events were to confirm that possibly, supported by the ease of travel between Preston and West Yorkshire along the M62 and M61 motorways.

The police newspaper carried details of Joan Harrison's killing. Was she really murdered by Wearside Jack?

Could Mrs Simpson provide more details on the possible identity of Wearside Jack? And would the sample of handwriting I had obtained from a potential "new suspect" eliminate him from inquiries? I visited Mrs Simpson in Chester to find out.

In her large home in the centre of Chester, Mrs Simpson has a file of samples of handwriting which were sent to her during the hunt for the Ripper/Wearside Jack. Some of the writing, she says, is surprisingly similar to that in the hoax letters.

Mrs Simpson, who has studied handwriting for 30 years, recalls the day she was asked to analyse the original hoax letters sent by Wearside Jack to George Oldfield.

She says: "My telephone rang in our office. It was a male voice and he said he was part of the Ripper Squad and he had been instructed by Assistant Chief Constable George Oldfield to ask me to look at some communications they had received.

"At this time, although we were in the North of England and we had heard a few bits and bobs about the murders, we were not aware that there was a Ripper Squad.

"He asked if he could come to see me and I agreed. Two police officers came to Chester with the alleged Ripper letters. One of the letters had been sent to the police and the other had been sent to a national newspaper. They were the original letters and I was also asked to look at the envelopes.

"All the material was bright pink, because all the paper had been through forensic testing. I was asked to produce a profile of the killer."

Handwriting expert Diane Simpson at her home in Chester. Picture: ***Patrick Lavelle.***

Mrs Simpson, a founder member of the British Institute of Graphologists, who has written three books on the subject of handwriting analysis, adds: "At the time I had just appeared in a television programme called 'Life Lines'. Forty programmes were made for four series. In the programme I was given writing, but not the identity of the writer, and I was asked to do a profile.

"The degree of accuracy I had obtained had impressed George Oldfield and he wanted to see if there were any clues which I could provide police with to help them with their inquiries.

"I was given the letters in April, 1979, and later they came with the envelope that had contained the tape. There was no doubt it was the same writer, but I did make the point to police at the time that the fact that it was the same handwriting on the envelopes did not mean that the same man had made the tape. They couldn't make that assumption.

"They told me they didn't want just anything I could give them, they wanted everything. I produced, to the best of my ability, a very detailed and very long profile of the writer. They took the report away with them and I did not keep a copy."

Mrs Simpson, who lectures in her specialist subject at Loughborough University, says that by taking certain measurements within the handwriting and by analysing the way the writer formed certain words, as well as measuring the pressure the writer put on the paper, she was able to come to certain conclusions about Wearside Jack.

She says: "The way it works is that I look at how the writing has changed since the way the writer had been taught to write. I look at the pressure in the writing. Graphology is a form of behavioural psychology. I would define it as the assessment of personality traits and likely behaviour through the analysis of the ways writing has been changed and adapted since the writer first learned to write."

Mrs Simpson recalls what she told Ripper Squad officers. She says: "I told them the writer had a high degree of manual dexterity. He may have been interested in electonics or assembling things. I pointed out that he was a working class type of chap and was more used to writing figures than letters.

"He was hyper-critical and, perhaps, sarcastic. As a personality type he was very unpleasant and negative. He liked the sound of his own voice and, I believe, he would have spoken out about the killings.

"His critical faculties were very well honed. He believed his opinion was slightly more superior than others and he was also a rather petty person. The writing was done quite quickly and it was not artificial. I refused to be drawn on the question as to whether or not the writer had committed those acts of violence."

She adds: "In one of the letters he mentioned the killing of Joan Harrison and linked the killing of Joan Harrison with the Ripper murders. I think that was the first time that link had been made.

"One of the main questions was, 'could this be the Yorkshire Ripper?' My response was that I had no way of knowing that.

"What the police were doing was surveying the whole situation. They wanted to know whether the letters and the tape should be taken seriously or whether they were 'just a joke'. The letters didn't follow the usual pattern of hoax letters."

After Mrs Simpson had provided police with her detailed report on Wearside Jack's handwriting she was invited to police headquarters at Millgarth, Leeds, by George Oldfield and the pair took part in a BBC television broadcast.

After the handwriting extracts were made public Mrs Simpson had one criticism of West Yorkshire Police. She had advised police that if they were to reproduce extracts of the handwriting the writing should be the same size as the original. The handwriting, says Mrs Simpson, was very small. However, West Yorkshire Police decided to enlarge the handwriting. Thus, it was a blown-up version of the original text that thousands of people across the country were shown.

Mrs Simpson says: "When we are comparing writing it's important we have it the same size. I suggested to the police that if they were going to reproduce the writing it had to be the actual size. They produced a newspaper handout which included part of the profile I had written. The police had enlarged the handwriting for clarity. It was not shown actual size."

After Mrs Simpson's involvement in the Ripper inquiry became known she was inundated with requests for handwriting analysis. Some people who suspected they knew Wearside Jack also sent her examples of their handwriting: "I had so many people bringing samples of writing to me. They all had the same question, 'Could this be the writer?'," she says.

So how would the samples of Jack's handwriting I had obtained back in the Wearside pub in March, 1999, compare to the handwriting in the original hoax letters sent by Wearside Jack to George Oldfield 20 years earlier?

After my first meeting with Jack, when he had printed his home address on an envelope, I compared his writing to that on a copy of one of the hoax letters. There were similarities in the way he formed certain letters, such as A, S, T and I.

However, after our second meeting when I had managed to obtain a copy of his handwriting in lower case or "longhand", I could see no real similarities to the handwriting of Wearside Jack. But mine was an untrained eye and it was Mrs Simpson who was the expert.

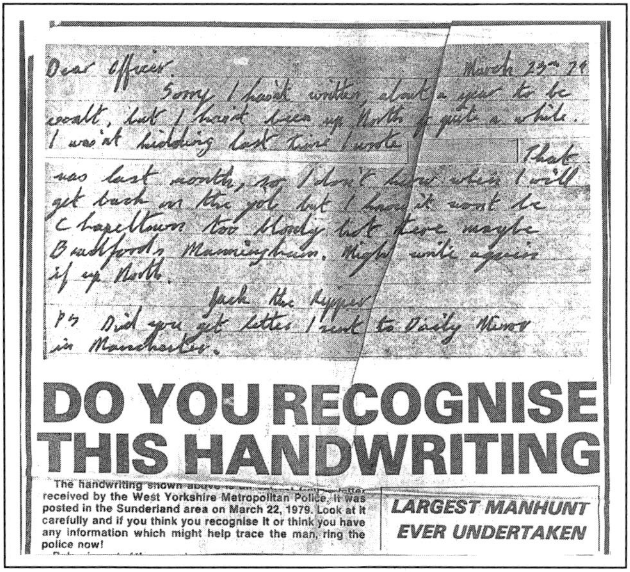

Dear Officer, March 23rd 79

Sorry I havn't written, about a year to be exact, but I havn't been up North for quite a while. I was'nt kidding last time I wrote

That was last month, so I don't know when I will get back on the job but I know it wont be Chapeltown too bloody hot there maybe Bradford's Manningham. Might write again if up North.

Jack the Ripper

PS Did you get letter I sent to Daily Mirror in Manchester.

DO YOU RECOGNISE THIS HANDWRITING

The handwriting shown above is ... letter received by the West Yorkshire Metropolitan Police. It was posted in the Sunderland area on March 22, 1979. Look at it carefully and if you think you recognise it or think you have any information which might help trace the man, ring the police now!

LARGEST MANHUNT EVER UNDERTAKEN

One of the extracts from one of the hoax letters showing Wearside Jack's handwriting. This appeared in the four-page "Help Us Catch The Ripper" newspaper produced by West Yorkshire Police. Handwriting expert Diane Simpson says the writing was reproduced larger than it actually was.

At her spacious office in Chester, surrounded by books on graphology, charts and handwriting samples, I handed Mrs Simpson the envelope Jack had addressed and the A4 lined sheet of paper on which he had written the words of a song.

Mrs Simpson took hold of her spectacles, which were hanging on a chain around her neck and put them on. She laid out the two pieces of paper on a desk in front of her, stood at the desk, and carefully examined Jack's handwriting. She sighed, took off her spectacles, turned to me and said: "No. It's very unlikely to be him. I would be amazed if it was him, even allowing for a gap of 20 years."

It was the answer I had, realistically, expected. Certain things Jack had told me in the pub during our second meeting suggested he was not the hoaxer. The handwriting analysis by Mrs Simpson had given me confirmation that Jack may be from Wearside, but he wasn't Wearside Jack.

Shortly afterwards I told Terry that his friend could not have been the hoaxer. Terry remained unconvinced: "Someone else may have written the letters for him," he said. That was possible, I thought, but very unlikely.

Jack was the same age as the suspect, his voice, even after 20 years, sounded like the voice on the hoax tape. He could recite the full contents of one of the hoax letters, said Terry, word perfect and as if he had rehearsed it. He probably had a tape recorder in 1979, might even have had a copy of the song *"Thank you for Being a Friend"* by Andrew Gold.

And there was one thing that Jack had told me that placed him in the same town at the same time that Joan Harrison - who, like Jack was a "down-and-out" who enjoyed a drink - had been so brutally killed. He had lived in Preston in 1975.

But the circumstantial evidence that pointed the finger of suspicion at Jack was nothing more, it appeared, than a series of coincidences that can put an innocent person in the frame for a crime they did not commit.

It was a series of coincidences that, 20 years earlier, had put many others in the frame as a possible suspect in the hunt for the Yorkshire Ripper/Wearside Jack. As several "suspects" have said, even now, as we approach a new millennium, some of their friends and colleagues may not have such strong suspicions about them being the hoaxer, but some still have niggling doubts.

If Jack, along with the thousands of other Sunderland men interviewed by police as potential suspects, was not Wearside Jack, who was he? Who was it that sent the chilling tape and the mocking letters to police that sent them on the biggest and most expensive wild goose chase in British criminal history and whose callous hoax probably cost the lives of three innocent women?

Who was the hoaxer of the century?

CHAPTER SEVENTEEN

Who Was Wearside Jack?

If the Yorkshire Ripper serial killings was the crime of the 20th century then the crime of the previous 100 years has to be the original Jack the Ripper murders in the East End of London in 1888. Like Sutcliffe, Jack had a down on "whores" or prostitutes. Both mutilated their victims and neither had sex with the women they killed. The big difference in the cases, of course, is that Sutcliffe was caught. Over the last 100 years there have been claims and speculation as to the identity of the original Jack the Ripper. But there has never been any firm evidence to substantiate those claims and the case remains shrouded in mystery and intrigue.

It is not known how many women were killed by Jack the Ripper but observers of the case - "Ripperologists" as they have become known - say he killed at least four, probably six and possibly as many as eight. It has been widely accepted that Jack's victims included Mary Ann Nichols, Annie Chapman, Elizabeth Stride, Catherine Eddowes and Mary Jane Kelly. All five women were murdered between August and November,1888; two of them, Catherine Eddowes and Elizabeth Stride, on the same date.

As with all notorious crimes, the Jack the Ripper case attracted the cranks, the mentally disturbed, the mischievous, and those callous individuals with malicious intent, who sent letters to Ripper Squad police claiming to be the "Whitechapel Fiend". There were hundreds of letters sent to police and the local Press and most experts on the case have dismissed them as hoaxes. However, there were three letters which many Ripperologists believe to have been genuine. One has become known as the "Dear Boss" letter, the second the "Saucy Jacky" postcard, and the third the "From Hell" letter.

With the permission of Stephen P Ryder, editor of *Casebook: Jack the Ripper* (http://ripper.wildnet.co.uk), the content of the three letters is reproduced here:

The "Dear Boss" letter was received by the Central News Agency in London on September 27, 1888, three days before the murders of Stride and Eddowes. It was the first time the title "Jack the Ripper" - the title Wearside Jack gave himself 90 years or so later - had been used. The letter said:

Dear Boss,

I keep on hearing the police have caught me but they wont fix me just yet. I have laughed when they look so clever and talk about being on the right track. That joke about Leather Apron gave me real fits. I am down on whores and I shant quit ripping them till I do get buckled. Grand work the last job was. I gave the lady no time to squeal. How can they catch me now. I love my work and want to start again. You will soon hear of me with my funny little games. I saved some of the proper red stuff in a ginger beer bottle over the last job to write with but it went thick like glue and I cant use it. Red ink is fit enough I hope ha ha. The next job I do I shall clip the ladys ears off and send to the police officers just for jolly wouldn't you. Keep this letter back till I do a bit more work, then give it out straight. My knife's so nice and sharp I want to get to work right away if I get a chance. Good luck.

Yours truly
Jack the Ripper

The "Saucy Jacky" postcard was received by the Central News Agency on October 1st, 1888. It said:

I was not codding dear old boss when I gave you the tip, you'll hear about saucy Jacky's work tomorrow double event this time number one squealed a bit couldn't finish straight off. Ha not the time to get ears for police. Thanks for keeping last letter back till I got to work again.

Jack the Ripper

The "From Hell" letter was received on October 16, 1888, by George Lusk, the president of the Whitechapel Vigilance Committee, inside a small cardboard box which also contained half a human kidney preserved in wine. The letter said:

From Hell.
Mr Lusk
Sor

I send you half the kidne I took from one woman and prasarved it for you tother piece I fried and ate it was very nise. I may send you the bloody knif that took it out if you only wate a whil longer.

Signed
Catch me if you can Mishter Lusk

The hoax letters sent to a news agency and handed to police in their hunt for Jack the Ripper in 1888 have nothing to do with the hoax letters sent to police in their hunt for the Yorkshire Ripper/Wearside Jack almost 90 years later. However, it is interesting to note that both sets were signed "Jack the Ripper", both were menacing and taunting and in both the writer claimed to be the serial killer. Both also wrote out "ha, ha" - laughing at what they perceived to be police ineptitude.

Ripper police in East London in 1888 did take one or two of the letters seriously, particularly the one where the writer told of a "double event" only a day after two of Jack the Ripper's victims met their deaths. Like the hoax letters sent to police in the Yorkshire Ripper inquiry, the writer appeared to know more about the killings than had been made public.

Most observers of the Jack the Ripper case believe all the letters to have been hoaxes. Neither Jack nor any of the hoax letter writers were ever caught.

Contemporary police artist's impression of Jack the Ripper. Illustration: *The Northern Echo.*

Jack's signature in a letter handed to police in 1888.

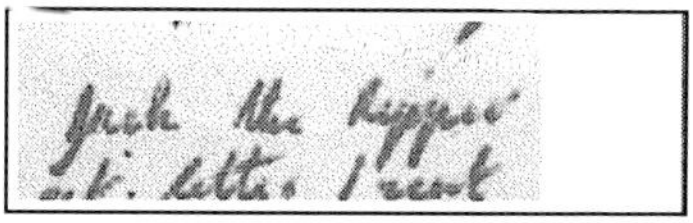

Wearside Jack's signature.

The Jack the Ripper case has excercised the minds of some of the most astute investigators and academics for more than a century. Interest in the case has not diminished over the years because it remains one of the greatest unsolved mysteries of the millennium.

If the inquiring minds of brilliant academics and some of the UK's top detectives over the space of 100 and more years have failed to unravel the Jack the Ripper mystery, what hope is there, realistically, of Wearside Jack ever being unmasked? As we approach the new millennium the chances of that happening appear remote.

Do people really give a damn whether or not Wearside Jack's identity is ever revealed?

I think they do.

Wearside Jack's hoax cast a shadow of suspicion and mistrust over the whole of Wearside. It had an impact on so many lives. The human cost far outweighs the £4million cost to police when they decided to switch the main focus of the Yorkshire Ripper inquiry to Sunderland. Three innocent women were killed when the hoaxer sent police on a false trail. What price a life?

North Shields grandmother Olive Curry still firmly believes she knows who Wearside Jack was and that he was an accomplice of the Yorkshire Ripper, assiting him in killing at least one of the victims. Now, in 1999, Mrs Curry is aged 70. Will she live to see Wearside Jack unmasked?

Her story is an intriguing one. She says she met Peter Sutcliffe and Jack at a canteen where she worked in North Shields in the mid to late 1970s. After seeing Sutcliffe's arrest on the television news she set off on what Sutcliffe later described as a "crusade". She befriended Sutcliffe, visited him in Broadmoor and has amassed hundreds of letters penned by the killer over a period of several years. She says her only motive in writing to Sutcliffe was to get him to admit to her claim that he knew Wearside Jack and that he was his accomplice.

Is that possible?

Mrs Curry has obviously gone to extreme lengths, and has spent a lot of her own money, in her pursuit of "the truth". Sutcliffe has constantly denied ever meeting her before or ever having met a man with a Sunderland accent and a lisp at the canteen where she worked. In 1993 detectives from West Yorkshire investigated Mrs Curry's claims and examined his work records. They concluded Sutcliffe could not have been in North Shields on the dates Mrs Curry had given them.

Might Mrs Curry have inadvertently given them the wrong dates? It is possible. And what should we believe; the word of arguably the most notorious serial killer this century or the word of a sensible and genuine 70-year-old woman who is unshakeable in her belief and determined to carry on with her "crusade"? What other possible motive could Mrs Curry have for befriending Peter Sutcliffe? Although Sutcliffe receives correspondence from many women across the country with a bizarre interest in him, Mrs Curry does not fit the usual profile of his female penpals.

Can we also believe Sutcliffe when he says he did not kill Joan Harrison in Preston in 1975? The forensic evidence at the scene did not put him in the frame. Mrs Curry believes that was one of the killings where Sutcliffe had an accomplice - whom she says was Wearside Jack. It is said that Sutcliffe's work records show he was in the area at the time of Mrs Harrison's killing. Is it possible that he did play a part in her murder, with an accomplice? Sutcliffe denied any involvement in the sending of the hoax letters and tape.

What about Terry's friend Jack? He was in Preston at the time of Mrs Harrison's murder and his voice does sound like the voice on the tape. There is also other circumstantial evidence against Jack. But he was interviewed by police and handwriting expert Diane Simpson, who analysed the original Wearside Jack hoax letters for police is convinced Jack is not the hoaxer. Terry, however, says he still believes Jack may have had something to do with it. If Wearside Jack did not kill Joan Harrison - and the evidence that he did is not that strong - the fact that Jack was in Preston at the time of her killing is of no significance.

Is there any evidence to back the suggestion that Wearside Jack was a police officer? In a book, published in 1996 the author went further than to suggest the hoaxer was a retired police officer. His statement was unequivocal: " ...Peter Sutcliffe was arrested on January 2, 1981 ... and was proved to be the Ripper, he bore little resemblance to the one who had made and sent the tape. The impostor turned out to be a retired policeman who had a grudge to settle with Inspector Oldfield," the author wrote. (John Douglas and Mark Olshaker. Mindhunter. Mandarin. 1996.)

Diane Simpson, who has kept a close eye on developments in the case since she analysed the hoax letters, says that statement has yet to be challenged by police in Northumbria, West Yorkshire or any other force. If that is so, why has police not yet issued a denial more than two years since that apparent statement of fact was published? It is unlikely that the book has not been read by any police officer and, if Mrs Simpson's assertion that no challenge has been forthcoming is correct, then the lack of a rebuttal can only fan the flames of speculation amongst those who would claim a cover-up.

During research for this book, one of the four names put forward as a possible Wearside Jack suspect was a retired police officer, still alive, and living on Wearside. The informant's suspicion was based only on the man's voice - he said he sounded like the man on the hoax tape - and there was nothing else to suggest the retired officer fitted the offender profile of the hoaxer, other than the fact he is from Wearside. Perhaps this line of inquiry warrants further research.

None of the "suspects" who have told their stories in this book are real suspects in the hunt for Wearside Jack. Some were only interviewed by Ripper Squad police because they happened to have Wearside accents and tenuous links with West Yorkshire. Others were the victims of a set of strange coincidences that put them in the wrong place, at the wrong time and with the wrong connections.

If Wearside Jack killed Joan Harrison his motive for sending the letters and tape were to shift blame for the killing onto Peter Sutcliffe. If the hoaxer was a retired police officer his motive may have been his dissatisfaction at how the inquiry was handled or he had a grudge against George Oldfield. If Wearside Jack was neither the killer of Mrs Harrison nor a retired police officer, then the hoax of the century appears motiveless and the hoaxer was nothing more than a sick individual with a warped sense of humour.

In the Jack the Ripper inquiry in the East End of London in 1888 it was suggested that at least one of the hoax letters was written by a journalist, intent of getting himself a big story. There has never been any suggestion that Wearside Jack was a North East journalist, though it is known that more than one newspaper reporter was interviewed, and eliminated, by police during the inquiry.

Was enough done by police to catch the hoaxer after the arrest of the Yorkshire Ripper?

Police from the Ripper Squad have given mixed views in answering that question. Some say a small team of detectives was kept on the case for a few months after the arrest of Sutcliffe but others say once the Ripper was caught the hoaxer was forgotten.

If, as one Ripper Squad detective claims, two hoax calls were made by Wearside Jack to the Tyne and Wear Fire Brigade in the months following the Ripper's arrest, it would have been an opportunity for police to issue a Press appeal for information from anyone who may have seen someone using the telephone kiosk at the time. No such appeals were made.

There was little publicity after the Ripper's arrest about the hunt for the hoaxer. As several Ripper Squad officers have said, it was a West Yorkshire police inquiry and they had caught the man they were looking for. Perhaps the apparent lack of resolve by police to catch the hoaxer was one of the reasons some people began asking whether the hoaxer was a police officer?

Whatever effort went into catching the hoaxer, police did not get a result.

If he is still alive the hoaxer of the century will be aged between 40 and 62. He will still have a strong Wearside accent and he is of the rare B secretor blood group. I wonder if he still has a copy of the Andrew Gold song *"Thank you for Being a Friend"*? The tape recorder he had in 1979 will now have become obsolete.

If handwriting can indicate the writer's personality - some would argue it can't - then, according to Diane Simpson, Wearside Jack is a sarcastic individual, unpleasant and negative, good with his hands, slightly supercilious, at times petty, hyper-critical and he likes the sound of his own voice. He is also working class.

If Wearside Jack did kill Joan Harrison in Preston in November, 1975, he has, or had, an eighth of an inch gap in his top two front teeth and he is a pervert. He also has or had links with prostitutes and travelled quite regularly from Wearside to other areas of the country. He was also, possibly, a down-and-out and a heavy drinker.

What do I think?

Perhaps after the months of spare-time research that has gone into producing this book I am entitled to speculate. But speculation it is. I do not know the identity of the hoaxer of the century. I can only guess.

WEST YORKSHIRE METROPOLITAN POLICE

5th JULY -79

£25,000 REWARD

A reward of £25,000 is offered for information leading to the arrest and conviction of the person (or persons) responsible for the above-mentioned crimes.

The sponsors are the West Yorkshire Metropolitan Police Authority who are offering up to £20,000 and Yorkshire Post Newspapers who are offering up to £5,000. The full terms under which this money is offered are as follows.—

RING FREEFONE 5050 OR CONTACT ANY POLICE OFFICER. WHAT YOU SAY WILL BE TREATED IN STRICTEST CONFIDENCE. YOUR IDENTITY WILL NOT BE REVEALED.

OR RING SUNDERLAND 43146.

THINK HARD AND COME FORWARD NOW IF YOU KNOW OR SUSPECT ANYTHING AT ALL, HOWEVER SMALL. IT COULD BE VITALLY IMPORTANT WHEN CONSIDERED WITH WHAT THE POLICE KNOW ALREADY.

Copies of this reward poster for the Yorkshire Ripper will be posted all round Wearside. The amount of £25,000 reward money has now been increased to £30,000.

Hundreds of these posters were distributed across Wearside in the hunt for the Yorkshire Ripper after police were sent a hoax tape and letters from a Sunderland man who claimed to be the serial killer. The reward eventually topped £30,000.

But, for what it's worth (bearing in mind I am not an "offender profiler" or an expert on the case), this is my guess.

I believe Wearside Jack is still alive and living on Wearside but has no family links with the north of Sunderland, generally, or Castletown, specifically. I think his family roots are on Wearside's border with County Durham and, though he has connections with the city of Sunderland, he does not consider Sunderland his home. I do not think he is a retired police officer.

Jack, I believe, has lived a nomadic existence and has never been able to keep a full-time job for long. He's a wanderer and he possibly began his travels after the death of his mother, to whom he was very close. He was probably not very close to his father, who may have been a strict disciplinarian, and he has probably never married or been involved in a long-term sexual relationship.

My guess is that Wearside Jack's father and grandfather worked in North East collieries and that he did have a "pitmatic" lilt to his voice. Jack became resentful towards women, after the death of his mother, and, after one or two failed attempts at forming relationships with local women, he turned his attention to working girls in the red light areas he occasionally visited in West Yorkshire.

I believe Jack, who had an inflated opinion of himself, was perceived by others to be a joke, but his skin was so thick he did not realise this. Jack also liked to drink and he liked the sound of his own voice. To some he appeared obnoxious, to others he was a "harmless character".

But Jack, I think, despite his unkempt appearance, still had self-esteem and the fact that he had to turn to prostitutes - having to pay for sex - because he could not form a normal relationship brought out his violent streak. And it was that, I guess, that led Jack to do something I also suspect he did ... kill Joan Harrison in Preston in November, 1975.

If he did kill Joan Harrison, he did so in a drunken rage and he came to regret it. He fled from Preston back to Wearside and the comfort and security of his "home" territory, where everyone knew him as a "bit of a laugh" and no one suspected him to be a killer.

And then he had a motive to write the hoax letters and record and send the hoax tape. He wanted to shift the blame for Mrs Harrison's murder onto Peter William Sutcliffe, the Yorkshire Ripper.

He posted the first two hoax letters - including one in which he mentioned the murder of Joan Harrison - near his home (most of Wearside at that time had a Sunderland postmark). But Ripper Squad police did not fully act on the letters in 1978 because Jack had failed to mention his latest victim, whose mutilated body had yet to be discovered.

Jack was worried. He read all the newspaper cuttings he could find on the Ripper killings and discovered, to his glee, that one of the victims was named as Vera Millward, who he remembered meeting when he visited the red light area of Manchester. He also recalled that Mrs Millward had told him about having treatment in a local hospital. Or, perhaps, he had read that in a local newspaper (Davey Zack always said everything in the letters could have been gleaned from newspaper reports).

Then, in March, 1979, in an effort to further convince police he was the Ripper, Jack wrote a third letter to police and mentioned his "meeting" with Mrs Millward. Three months later the tape followed and the hunt for Wearside Jack fully switched to Wearside.

But then came the Castletown connection and a false trail, within a false trail.

However, Wearside Jack became very nervous as the net appeared to be closing in. And he started his adventures once more, travelling from Wearside to West Yorkshire, Lancashire or anywhere else he was little known.

He was never interviewed at length by Ripper Squad police, but may have been questioned. He never gave police a sample of his saliva, in Preston in 1975 or on Wearside between 1979 and early 1981, and probably never gave them a sample of his handwriting or a recording of his voice.

And, after the hunt for the hoaxer appeared to fizzle out following the arrest of Peter Sutcliffe, Wearside Jack, quietly but deliberately drifted back into his nomadic, obscure, pathetic life, believing he had put the past firmly behind him.

But has he?

My outline of what I guess might have happened is only a guess. I do not claim to have any inside knowledge on the case of Wearside Jack other than that which has been made public in this book.

But there is one thing I know to be true. And it is this.

The people of Wearside have long been known to have a resilient nature. They can laugh in the face of adversity, and get on with their lives.

But Wearside Jack and the hoax of the century? That is something else.

My only hope is that some of the information in this book, made public for the first time in 20 years, might just lead to him being identified and brought to justice.

The hoaxer of the century has a massive debt to repay the people of Wearside. It is time to settle the debt.

BIBLIOGRAPHY

Brian Lane and Wilfred Gregg	1992	The Encyclopedia of Serial Killers. Headline Book Publishing plc.
John Douglas and Mark Olshaker	1996	Mindhunter. Mandarin.

NEWSPAPERS

The Sunderland Echo
The Northern Echo
The Yorkshire Post
The Yorkshire Evening Press
The Lancashire Evening Post
Daily Mail

OTHER SOURCES

Stephen P Ryder	Casebook: Jack the Ripper	http://ripper.wildnet.co.uk

THE AUTHOR

Patrick Lavelle is a 39-year-old journalist working for the *Sunderland Echo*. He lives in Sunderland with his partner, Maureen, and their son, Tom. He has worked in journalism in the North East of England for 13 years. He was the North East Investigative Journalist of the Year in the Tom Cordner Press Awards, 1994. He graduated from the University of Northumbria, Newcastle Upon Tyne, in June, 1998, with a degree in Criminal Justice Studies/Criminology. This is his first book.

Patrick Lavelle

Picture: ***Malcolm Murray. The Sunderland Echo.***